This book is for

_____

⚬

f**P**

My Hero

*Extraordinary People
on the Heroes
Who Inspire Them*

EDITED BY

The My Hero Project

INTRODUCTION BY

Earvin "Magic" Johnson

FREE PRESS
NEW YORK LONDON TORONTO SYDNEY

FREE PRESS

A Division of Simon & Schuster, Inc.

1230 Avenue of the Americas

New York, NY 10020

For information about special discounts for bulk purchases,
please contact Simon & Schuster Special Sales:
1-800-456-6798 or business@simonandschuster.com

Designed by Joe Rutt

Manufactured in the United States of America

1 3 5 7 9 10 8 6 4 2

Library of Congress Cataloging-in-Publication Data
  My hero: extraordinary people on the heroes who inspire them / edited by
the My Hero Project; introduction by Earvin "Magic" Johnson.
     p. cm.
  1. Heroes—Biography. 2. Inspiration. I. My Hero Project.
II. Title.
CT 105 .M89 2005
920.073 B—dc22   2005052192

ISBN-13: 978-0-7432-8345-8
ISBN-10:   0-7432-8345-7

We dedicate this book to our parents, grandparents, and teachers—who led by example, encouraging us to always follow our dreams. It is also dedicated to our children—who inspire, nag, and challenge us each day to make the world a better place.

—KP, JM, RS

Contents

Foreword by Karen Pritzker
for The My Hero Project   *xi*

Introduction by
Earvin "Magic" Johnson   *xvii*

Muhammad Ali   *1*

Dr. Robert Ballard   *5*

Yogi Berra   *10*

Sue Bird   *16*

Senator Bill Bradley   *20*

Reverend Doctor Calvin O. Butts, III   *25*

Richard "Bo" Dietl   *32*

Dr. Felton Earls   *36*

Kathy Eldon   *44*

Michael J. Fox   *50*

Frank O. Gehry 54

Mayor Rudolph Giuliani 58

Senator John Glenn 61

Erin Gruwell 67

Scott Hamilton 72

Ralf Hotchkiss 78

Colonel Jack Jacobs,
   U.S. Army (Retired) 83

Billie Jean King 90

Sherry Lansing 96

Frances Moore Lappé 103

Leon Lederman 109

Stan Lee 114

Congressman John Lewis 118

Dr. Bernard Lown 126

Wangari Maathai 134

Wynton Marsalis 139

Senator John McCain 144

Ralph Nader 151

Paul Newman *156*

Stan O'Neal *159*

Raffi *163*

Ron Reagan *167*

Dana Reeve *171*

Paul Rusesabagina *178*

Dennis Smith *186*

Jeni Stepanek *192*

Vivian Stringer *196*

Rob Warden *202*

Elie Wiesel *208*

Acknowledgments *215*

*Charitable Organizations Supported
by Contributors to* My Hero *221*

Tell the World About Your *Hero* *227*

About The My Hero Project *229*

About the Introduction Author *231*

Foreword

How far that little candle throws his beams!
So shines a good deed in a naughty world.
—William Shakespeare

In the late summer of 1968, I watched from my bedroom window as police in riot gear battled protesters and bystanders in Chicago's Lincoln Park. Earlier that spring, I'd heard my parents talk in hushed voices about the assassination of Martin Luther King, Jr. The jungles of Vietnam burned nightly on our TV screens, and the aftermath of Richard Speck's murderous rampage—eight nurses killed right in my neighborhood—continued to dominate the front pages of the newspaper.

Those were turbulent and violent times, especially confusing for a fourth-grader. But I was fortunate, because what I recall most vividly from my childhood are not these violent images, but the stories of bravery, generosity, and heroic endeavor shared by my parents and their friends around our dinner table. It was there that my siblings and I heard about a white manufacturer who refused to build a factory in the South with two separate sets of water fountains and bathrooms for "coloreds" and whites, and a woman who left her sorority in protest because they opposed her having a Japanese boyfriend. I sat spellbound as a Jewish visitor told us how a Christian family rescued him from a war-torn Poland, raised him, and then returned him to his mother's arms after World War II was over.

Stories like these (and there were many more) showed me how courageous, honorable, giving, and fair people could be even—perhaps especially—in bad times. Hearing these tales, I imagined myself in the shoes of the people described, confronted by similar challenges, and I hoped I'd make similarly courageous choices.

I was ten when I got the idea of starting a "good news" newspaper, filled strictly with news of good works. I realized even then that real-life stories of sacrifice, heroism, and courage make great copy. My good newspaper would trumpet the best of humanity and provide a counterpoint to the "if it bleeds, it leads" ethic that buries good news in the back pages.

I grew up, and my dream of a good news newspaper got tabled, as dreams sometimes do. But even as I went on to a career in journalism and a family of my own, the idea stayed with me. The chance to realize this childhood dream came in the mid-nineties, when two friends, the accomplished film-

makers Jeanne Meyers and Rita Stern, approached me about
My Hero.

They were mothers of young children at the time, as was I,
and like most parents, eager to make the world a better place
for their kids. Specifically, they were concerned that traditional heroes were conspicuously absent from the great grab
bag of popular culture offered to our kids, eclipsed by super-
heroes, pop stars, and celebrities. Jeanne and Rita's point was
that heroes were still all around us, but they weren't getting
airtime.

Their solution: a web site called myhero.com, which
would celebrate heroes and heroism. Here children and their
parents could read and post stories of courage and inspiration to share with people around the world. This truly was
my good news newspaper—only better.

The mission of the My Hero web site is to spotlight real-
life stories that "Celebrate the Best of Humanity." That's
what visitors have been doing since 1995. My hero.com now
welcomes more than a million visitors each month. Clearly
we weren't the only ones starving for some good news!

The stories we receive from visitors to our web site testify
to the fact that heroism comes in many shapes, sometimes
unexpected. They also remind us of the boundless generosity
and goodwill of our fellow men and women. Kids often write
about their favorite sports idols, civil rights leaders, musicians, and movie stars. Yet there is also an unending stream of

tributes paid to unsung heroes: neighbors, grandparents, nurses, or that special teacher, and, in one instance, a sister who had declared a temporary cease-fire in a particularly bitter sibling dispute—just long enough to donate her kidney to the brother who'd have died without it.

One of the privileges of working on the web site is to have a ringside seat at a steady stream of stories about remarkable heroes. Reading these sparked a question that was the catalyst for this book: "Who inspires the heroes who so inspire the rest of us?" From what reservoir do our heroes draw *their* strength and inspiration?

As you will see in the pages that follow, we have gathered a broad spectrum of contributors. Included here are military heroes, first responders, and sports greats, Nobel Prize recipients, legendary artists, and world-class scientists; world leaders and ordinary people who have done extraordinary things. Our contributors come from all walks of life and from around the globe, but if they have one thing in common, it's this: Because of them the world is richer and brighter. These are the people who have inspired us and others, by word, action, and deed. In this book, they share stories about the people who inspired *them*.

If we have learned anything from the stories collected in this book, it's that a single stone thrown in a pond can produce ripples that will extend farther than anyone can imagine at the moment of impact. An act of heroism isn't quantifiable; there's no measure of the lives it will touch. No matter who our contributors chose as heros, or why, their choices reveal how their own paths were illuminated, and by doing so shed precious light on our own.

Karen Pritzker

for The My Hero Project

Introduction

I believe in the power of heroes.

What is a hero? There are as many different answers to that question as there are people in the world, and that's a good thing: we need different kinds of role models for different kinds of people. I personally think a hero is a leader who has a positive impact on people. A hero is someone who acts and through those actions changes the world.

Sometimes heroes make their impact by giving a voice to people who don't have one, or by helping people to help themselves. That's a powerful form of heroism for me. If nobody believes in you enough to show you the way, to guide and encourage you, then why would you invest in yourself? Just knowing that someone else cares can make you care too.

Hope is everything. Before you can achieve anything, you have to have a dream: as I like to say, "You have to dream it to do it." We need heroes to show us what's possible, through their words or by example. Watching Bill Russell showed me the kind of basketball player I wanted to be: a player who shared the ball and the credit for a win with his teammates. Spending time with Jerry Buss taught me what kind of businessman I wanted to be: a man of his word who treats people with compassion and respect, and someone who gives back to the community. Most important, watching my father night after night in my family's home showed me the kind of man I wanted to be: a loving husband and a good father who always works hard and does the right thing.

When people think of heroes, they often think first of world leaders, people from the history books or in the public eye. I would never take away from the impact that some of those people have had; I list Martin Luther King, Jr., who stood up for our rights through nonviolence and lost his life for what he believed in, as one of mine. But, as you'll see over and over in this book, sometimes the most effective heroes are local people you can meet and see and talk to. I first learned about business from Greg Eaton and Joel Ferguson in Lansing, Michigan—the first African-Americans I ever met who owned their own businesses. They sat with me and shared their own stories, answered my questions, and encouraged my dreams. "I want to be like them," I thought, and seeing what they had accomplished gave me hope.

By educating and encouraging us, whether personally or just by example, our heroes help us make our dreams realities. Every successful person needed some help to get there. For me, the real heroes are the people who remember that when they arrive. A hero turns around, looks back at where he came from, and asks what he can do to bring other people along so that they can realize their own dreams. A hero does what he can to create other leaders, never forgetting that once upon a time, he was the one with the outstretched hand.

The imprint our heroes make on us stays with us forever. When I was growing up, my mother always taught me how important it is to share your blessings. As a kid, that meant shoveling other people's driveways without payment, even though I needed that dollar! Now, sharing my blessings means all the work we do through the Magic Johnson Foundation: building clinics and giving scholarships and bringing opportunities to neighborhoods that other people thought could never change. There's not a day that goes by in my life that I don't use something my parents gave me, and I hope that my own children will be able to say the same thing about me.

We don't have to look far and wide for our heroes; they're all around us. I'm proud to raise the money to build clinics to help children with HIV/AIDS, but to me, the true heroes are the kids who struggle every day with the disease and the doctors and nurses who care for them. I'm glad I can provide college scholarships to kids who couldn't otherwise afford it, but it's the little girl who does her homework lying flat on her belly on the floor to avoid stray bullets from drive-by shootings in her neighborhood who really earns my respect. Where people saw a blighted urban wasteland, I saw communities that needed movie theaters and coffee shops like any other community—and I am inspired by the members of those communities who have come together heroically to make that dream happen.

We'll always need heroes. We need people to help kids stay in school and ways to help them pay for college, and we need kids with the drive and dedication to go. It will take heroes to make sure that revitalized neighborhoods continue to flourish for the next generation and the ones after that. In particular, I see how badly we need heroes in minority communities.

As a society, we need to put heroes front and center. We need to show respect for people who have done great things and done them the right way, with integrity and hard work. We need to support people who care about other people and who will invest in our youth and our communities. We need to learn from those who have the courage and strength to take a unpopular stand and meet the consequences head-on. In the pages that follow, you'll find many of these stories. I hope they inspire you as they have inspired me.

When heroes act, they take the concept of hope and they make it real, something you can see and feel and touch. We all have the power to be a hero within us. If every one of us grabs the opportunity to make a difference, we're going to hear a whole lot more children saying "I have a chance," and that's the kind of change that can change the world.

Muhammad Ali

"Float like a butterfly, sting like a bee . . ."

During the 1996 Atlanta Summer Olympics, the world looked on as a determined Muhammad Ali accepted the Olympic torch and, with hands shaking from the effects of Parkinson's disease, lit the flame that would burn throughout the sixteen-day event. It was just one of the many times the legendary boxer and humanitarian has lit up the world.

In a career that included 56 wins, three world championships, and a gold medal from the 1960 Rome Olympics, Ali demonstrated not just pure power and athleticism, but bravery, integrity, and a generosity that transcends athletics, race, religion, and politics. In addition to his prowess in the ring, Ali dedicated his life to fighting for his own and others' civil rights.

With his legendary charm, wit, and steadfast allegiance to his principles, Ali has become an iconic figure who inspires those who share his personal views—and those who don't. Beloved and respected around the globe, he has made an impact on many continents. Just before the start of the first Gulf War, for example, Ali negotiated the release of fifteen hostages held in Iraq. He has been honored as a United Nations Messenger of Peace and is a major contributor to numerous humanitarian causes throughout the world, donating both publicly and anonymously. In 2005, the Muhammad Ali Center opened its doors in Louisville, Kentucky, to help young people "find greatness within," by focusing on the themes that have carried Ali so gracefully through his own life: confidence, conviction, dedication, respect, spirituality, and generosity.

Nelson Mandela is my hero. His story has come to symbolize the struggle against the apartheid machine in South Africa. Apartheid, the terrible, and often violent, institutionalized racism that for so long held South African society in its grip, was not an easy policy to fight against—especially since he was oppressed within the system. Mandela understands what it means to fight against enormous odds; he went to prison for nearly three decades for his work, because he knew there was no alternative. He believes that every human being is of equal value.

Mandela is my hero because he survived many years of life as a subject of colonialism. As a child in Africa, Mandela was a victim of the European colonial project that involved "civilizing" indigenous folks by silencing African lifeways in favor of so-called Eurocentric high culture. Perhaps finding his Xhosa name, Rolihlahla, too cumbersome or primitive, a teacher assigned him the decidedly more English "Nelson" when he was a student at a British colonial boarding school.

Mandela is my hero because he embraces all people like brothers and sisters. He is one of the greatest civil rights leaders in world history. Mandela is my hero because his spirit cannot be crushed. Imprisoned for his political views in the early 1960s, Mandela refused to compromise his position, which was equality and justice for all people. He sacrificed his own freedom for the self-determination of all South Africans. He is courageous and uncompromising.

Mandela is my hero because he is a man of great personal honor, strength, and integrity, but he was always fighting for something greater than himself, and that was the freedom of an entire nation. It is painful to imagine that this man, who radiates so much love, who espoused so many truths, could have spent so much of his life in prison.

Mandela is my hero because he triumphed over injustice, and not in a small way. Almost unimaginable just a few years before, Nelson Mandela became the first democratically elected president of South Africa in 1994 and served in that position for five years.

More than anyone in the world, Mandela embodies the hopes and dreams of a true, lasting justice and equality, not just for South Africans but for all people. It is Mandela—

through his unselfish and constant presence on the international stage raising awareness about AIDS, peace, debt relief, the environment—who most inspires us to think responsibly of our fellow man and of our planet.

Nelson Mandela has always inspired me to think beyond myself, to think of people in the wider world as part of a common humanity. I am blessed by his friendship. I love him for what he has accomplished, for what he has been through, for his journey forward. He remains a hallmark of what it *really* means to give of oneself selflessly—which is, indeed, a gift for us all.

Muhammad Ali

Dr. Robert Ballard

There's something about Dr. Robert Ballard that brings out the inner nine-year-old in all of us. Maybe it's his stories of discovering buried treasure, giant worms, and underwater volcanoes. Or the robot submarines he designed to explore the sunken decks of the Lusitania, the Bismarck, and Brittanica. Or the fact that he descended 12,000 feet in 1985 to find one of the most famous shipwrecks in history, the RMS Titanic.

With over a hundred deep-sea expeditions to his credit, Ballard moves through the underwater landscape with the precision of a scientist and the excitement of an explorer. His new work in the Black Sea has unearthed ships that date to the time of Ancient Greece and the Phoenician trade routes. This legendary oceanographer is also the founder of JASON, a project that allows hundreds of thousands of children to learn about deep-sea exploration interactively. In this way, Ballard is able to share his sense of wonder and discovery with a whole new generation of explorers.

The desire to explore is the most natural thing in the world. We're born with it. Can you imagine spending your whole life in a closed room, without ever trying the knob on the door? Not a chance! You'll jiggle that handle at the first opportunity. Unfortunately, too often in childhood, the pilot light of our curiosity gets blown out. I was lucky; mine never did. I grew up in San Diego, surrounded by the sea, and I was obsessed with movies like *20,000 Leagues Under the Sea, Journey Beneath the Sea, Sea Hunt, Mr. Peabody and the Mermaid,* and *Creature from the Black Lagoon.* I dreamt of travel and exploration, of great journeys and discoveries. Many of the characters I was introduced to then became my heroes, and remain so today: Jason and his Argonauts, Odysseus, Captain Nemo, and Captain James Cook. Mythical or real, they were all great explorers, and all of them were larger than life. My heroes weren't perfect, but I think there's something to be learned from the more flawed aspects of their personalities as well. Most of them didn't ride into the sunset with a "Happily Ever After." Cook died because he made a mistake. He turned his back, and got into a situation from which he couldn't extract himself. Jason's wife killed their children after he betrayed her. Nemo, fictional though he may be, was a very angry man. He didn't process the anger, and it consumed him. Those are things to watch out for.

If I had to distill the one thing that I've learned from my heroes, it would be leadership. All of these men were great leaders. I always find myself asking, how did they get people to follow them into harm's way—and how did they bring them back alive? Cook was proud of how few men he lost. A forty percent mortality rate was standard on most crews, but the numbers on his ships were much, much smaller. He worried about the people under his command, and took care of them. That, to me, is the sign of a great leader. Tragically, huge numbers of his crew died later of disease in the Dutch Indies; it broke his heart.

Joseph Campbell (another one of my heroes, an explorer of the mind) has said that life is "the act of becoming"; one never arrives. Everyone's on a journey, making a trip through time and space. Explorers—like Jason, and Odysseus, and Captain Cook—just do it in an orchestrated way. Their journeys are epic ones. I have found that their journeys have a predictable pattern to them, and I have found, over the course of my life, that mine have, as well.

All the great journeys begin with a dream. Christopher Columbus said, "I want to find a western route to India." For Jason, it was the Golden Fleece. For me, it was the *Titanic*. That dream is the driving force, the impetus, the quest. Life is a giant quest, and in many cases, we never get the answer. But that should never extinguish the desire to know.

Once you've embarked on your journey, that's when you

discover how important preparation is, because Neptune will always test you. All of my heroes were tested. It took Odysseus ten years to get home! Preparation has a lot to do with how you survive that test. When you read Cook's journals, you see a committed, intelligent, disciplined, patriotic man; I admire those qualities in him. He did his homework. And he was cool under fire, which is a necessity when you lead; for an explorer, it can often mean the difference between life and death. But it takes more than preparation or a cool head, because the hardest part of Neptune's test is always the test of your heart, your passion.

My heroes have taught me that failure is a given, and it is the greatest teacher you'll ever meet. The real question isn't "How can I make it through life without screwing up," but "What will I do when that happens?" Will I—*can* I—process the failure? Odysseus had enough passion to keep getting back up off the mat, no matter how many times he was knocked down. Jason had it, Cook had it, and Nemo had it. You have to have it, in order to pass the test.

When the test is passed, Neptune pulls back the veil of secrecy and there's the truth. But the quest is not yet finished. As far as I'm concerned, the journey of a true explorer is not over until you have shared the truth you have discovered with the world. That's what an explorer does—he comes back, and communicates what he's learned. He educates. He doesn't just say, "I had a great time." He says, "I collected all this information, and I made all these maps, and I brought back something to share with society." That process is vitally important, not just for the society it enriches, but for the explorer. Sharing what he's learned releases him, so that he can dream again. That's one of the reasons that I'm a big believer in passing the torch. There's no question in my mind that the golden age of exploration is in front of us, not behind us. We're reaching out with the Hubble telescope to the edge of the big bang. We're probing the moons of Saturn. We're looking for life on Mars. There's a staggering amount still to learn, just about the inside of the human body alone. New frontiers are everywhere we look.

The next generation is going to smoke us. They're going to blow us out of the water the way we blew our parents' generation away. The school kids that I talk to, the graduate students who come out to sea with me—they're the next Odysseuses, the next Cooks. It's an honor to think that a story I tell them or something I can show them might inspire them the way the stories of Jason and Nemo inspired me. Because these kids are going to go where no one has gone before. They're going to stand on our shoulders and see things we never dreamed of seeing—and I, for one, can't wait.

Yogi Berra

Yogi Berra is an American original, almost as renowned for his inimitable philosophy as he is for his baseball brilliance. No other sports figure has more entries in Bartlett's Familiar Quotations, *and no other player in the history of baseball has won more championship rings. Yet what truly makes him a beloved national treasure may be his humility, kindness, and genuineness.*

Perhaps no more unlikely-looking an athlete ever strode onto a playing field. In fact, Yogi's squat, gnome-like body inspired caricature and jokes. Yet there was nothing funny about how he rose from barefoot sandlotter to Hall of Fame heights as catcher for the New York Yankees and one of the greatest dynasties in sports history.

Lawrence Peter Berra, the son of Italian immigrants, was born in St. Louis on May 12, 1925. He got his nickname when some of his childhood buddies saw a resemblance between him and an Indian fakir they'd seen in a movie. Though he quit school at age 14 to help support his family, he had a genius for playing the game that transcended his physical configuration. His unlikely baseball odyssey was interrupted by World War II, when he served in the Navy and participated in the D-Day invasion of Omaha Beach on June 6, 1944.

In a playing career that spanned 17 full seasons (1947–63) and the "Golden Age of Baseball," he appeared in a record 14 World Series, 10 of which the Yankees won. Astonishingly agile defensively, he was also one of the game's greatest clutch hitters and won the Most Valuable Player Award in the American League three times. As a manager, he won pennants in both leagues, with the Yankees in 1964 and the Mets in 1973.

Despite becoming a national celebrity, he's been delightfully unchanged by it all. He's faithfully devoted to his wife of 56 years, Carmen, and the rest of his family, which includes three sons and 10 grandchildren. The values reflected in his life and accomplishments—respect, tolerance, and sportsmanship—inspired the creation of the Yogi Berra Museum & Learning Center, on the campus of Montclair State University in New Jersey, in 1998.

Where I came from in St. Louis is called The Hill. It's strictly an Italian neighborhood, most people there came from the Old Country. My pop, Pietro, was one of them. He came from Malvaglio, a little town in northern Italy, around 1913. He couldn't speak much English. But he found steady work as a laborer in the brickyard, and coming from where he came from, felt lucky to have it.

The Hill was no slum. It was a respectable neighborhood. People worked hard and lived in small, brick bungalows. Those houses were handed down to family members, generation to generation, and still are. To me, the Hill will always be a special place, where family and church and sports were the important things. It's where my Pop worked hard trying to support us five kids—Tony, Mike, John, me, and my younger sister, Josie. Today, Josie still lives in the Hill, in our old house at 5447 Elizabeth Ave.

Pop was the boss. He had rules and you'd better obey them. If you were late for Mass or forgot to go to Confession on Saturday afternoon, you'd catch heck. With Pop you better live up to your word. Tell him you'll be home a certain time, you better be there. Like when the 4:30 whistle blew at the Laclede-Christy brickworks. My job was to run to the tavern to get a tankard of beer for him and bring it home. If the beer wasn't on the table waiting for him, I'd be in trouble, and I knew it.

He never liked me playing ball. Being from the Old Country, he still wasn't used to the ways of America. He didn't believe you could make an honest dollar chasing after balls with a stick and a glove. "Baseball? A bum's game," he'd say. He'd always get mad if I came home dirty or with torn pants.

All the kids on The Hill lived for sports. We played in the street, in the schoolyard, and in the park. We played every game there was, soccer, baseball, corkball, football, even boxing.

Of course, things got a bit tough during the Depression. Money was something you had to think about a lot. It bothered Pop that my brothers were more interested in playing than working. They were all real good ballplayers, too. Tony was the oldest, everyone called him "Lefty." He was a pitcher and outfielder, the best player on The Hill, and the Cleveland Indians wanted to sign him. But Pop said "No" and no it was. So Tony went to work in Ward's bakery. Mike and John were also real good amateur players—both the St. Louis Cardinals and Browns were interested in them. But Pop would have none of it. Mike got a job in the shoe factory and John waited tables at Ruggieri's. To Pop, these were honest jobs, something to depend on.

I still remember watching my brothers play—they were gifted players. When I was about 12 or 13 they played a barnstorming black team whose catcher was Josh Gibson. Mostly, though, I loved to play and that's all I did. Me and Joe Garagiola, my buddy from across the street, organized a sports club called the Stags. We used splintered bats and taped-up balls and we played and played.

I didn't care much for school in those days. So after the eighth grade, I quit to go to work, like my older brothers. I worked in a coal yard, on a Coca-Cola truck, and Mike helped my get a job at the Johansen shoe factory. It helped put a few dollars in the household. But I never kept a job for long—it interfered with my ballplaying. I was playing American Legion ball when I was 15, that's when I first got the nickname "Yogi." A couple of years later, my Legion manager Leo Browne arranged for me to try out with the St. Louis Cardinals. But Branch Rickey, who was running the Cardinals, wouldn't give me a $500 signing bonus he gave to Garagiola. I thought I was doomed to work in some shop or factory, like my brothers.

But after the 1942 season, Browne told John Schulte, a Yankee coach who came from St. Louis, that the Yankees could sign me for $500. Schulte was going to come to our house with a contract. I couldn't have been more excited, or more depressed since I knew Pop wouldn't go for it.

I rushed home to talk to my brothers. That night after dinner, Tony, Mike, and John had a long argument with Pop. They lobbied hard for me, saying it's what I had to do, it's my life, it's my chance. They kept saying baseball was a business, people pay to see it. And look at DiMaggio, he's Italian and making good money playing baseball.

My brothers might've been better players than me. But I was the lucky one. They ganged up on Pop that night, pleading with him to give me the chance they never got. They even told him they'd work extra to bring home more money to make up for me. When Pop finally said yes, my life changed forever.

When someone asks me about my heroes that's easy: It's Tony, Mike, and John, my older brothers. I've never forgotten their sacrifices. Not only of their own dreams, but of their efforts on my behalf. They were good men, dedicated to family their whole lives. They are all gone but I remain indebted. During my playing days with the Yankees, I once told Pop if he had let my brothers play he would've been a millionaire. He said, "Blame your mother."

Yogi Berra

Sue Bird

Sue Bird has always been an extraordinary athlete and competitor. Even as a very young child, she blew everyone away—boys included!—on the track and the soccer field, but she truly blossomed when she discovered basketball.

In her senior year of high school, she led the powerhouse Christ the King High School in an undefeated season, and was named the New York City/State Player of the Year. By the time she'd graduated from the University of Connecticut, she'd taken the team to two NCAA championships and won pretty much every individual award offered in the sport. The number one draft pick of the 2002 WNBA, Bird was snapped up to play starting point guard for the Seattle Storm, and in her first year with the team, she took it to its first playoff appearance ever. She also took home a gold medal from the 2004 Olympics in Athens, as a member of the USA women's basketball team.

Bird is known not just for her extraordinary athleticism, intelligence, competitive spirit, and versatility, but for her generos-

ity toward her teammates on the court. That generosity extends off the court to her thousands of fans, making her a natural ambassador for the sport.

In choosing an "official" hero, I thought I should probably do a mental scan through my personal catalogue of luminary figures—but that didn't work. The truth is that I simply couldn't get one name out of my head, and that one name was drowning out all the rest. It was the first name that popped into my head when asked who my hero is. That name belongs to Jennifer Bird, my older sister.

So, although I felt like I somehow *ought* to choose amongst the coaches, teammates, and legendary sports figures who have all influenced me in important ways—none of these in the end are my one true hero. Jen is.

Why? For so many reasons, I could probably fill an entire book. She is caring, kind, and intelligent. But most of all, she's *real*—with no pretensions, and no airs. She never loses sight of who she is. That's something I've really tried to learn from her. For instance, I had many college scholarship opportunities, and a number of people were pushing me to choose Stanford, one of the best universities in the country, or Vanderbilt, which is also an excellent academic institution. But when I visited the University of Connecticut, I knew that the University of Connecticut and head coach

Gino Auriemma would be the best fit for me, both athleti-
cally and academically. Even though there was quite a bit of
pressure for me to choose one of the other schools because
they're perceived as stronger academically, I followed Jen's example and stayed true to myself, even if that meant taking a
risk. It was absolutely the right choice, and I owe it to Jen.

For me, heroism, and the true measure of a person's character, is all about how you handle adversity. "When the going
gets tough, the tough get going." My whole family actually
scores high points in this regard, but Jen takes the cake. She's
always steady, no matter what ups and downs life serves up. I
admire this about her.

Maybe the most significant contribution that Jen has
made to my life is that she has taught me—by word and
example—how to be a role model. When Jen and I were
younger, I idolized her. I was the little sister who wanted to
do what she did, wear what she was wearing, and play the
same sports that she played—like basketball. Admiring
someone like that is a very powerful thing, and I'm not sure
how common it is to find admiration between siblings. I was
in competition with her, as many sisters are, but in my case I
think it was more about being good enough to make her
proud than it was about beating her.

As a sports figure with a high profile, I am aware that
many young girls and boys now consider me to be *their* hero.
It's something I am really proud of. When I grew up, there

weren't very many female athletes on television or in the news, so the athletes that I looked up to as a little girl were mostly male. There is nothing wrong with that, but I think it's really important for girls and boys to be able to see female athletes on ESPN and the other networks, playing professional sports. Little girls may still be influenced by male athletes—or musicians, teachers, or their parents, for that matter—but now they'll at least have the choice. I'm proud to have been part of this transformation in the sports world, and whatever positive impact that change might have made on us as a nation.

It is a wonderful honor to be a role model, but I also recognize the responsibility that comes with it. I'm reminded of that responsibility every time I open fan mail from all over the world, or see someone wearing my jersey in the stands, or sign a ball for a little girl. For me to remain deserving of this role, I know the key thing is *to stay myself*—a middle-class girl who grew up a tomboy, just playing the game I love. No matter how great my accomplishments on the basketball court, what counts is that I stay grounded and humble in my pursuits. That's what Jennifer taught me.

Thank you, Jen. You will always be my hero.

Senator Bill Bradley

A three-time basketball All-American at Princeton University in the 1960s, and Olympic gold medalist, Bill Bradley turned down a chance to play professional basketball to attend Oxford as a Rhodes scholar. He studied politics, philosophy, and economics for two years . . . then returned to the game. He signed a contract with the New York Knicks and built a distinguished ten-year career that garnered two NBA championships and election to the Basketball Hall of Fame.

Next this scholar-athlete turned his talents to public service. In 1978 he won an open U.S. Senate seat in New Jersey, where he turned his eye to energy (especially the California water crisis), tax issues, and NAFTA. Elected to three terms, he earned a reputation in the Senate as a nonpartisan statesman who attacked issues with the same characteristic persistence and drive that he displayed on the basketball court. Senator Bradley distinguished himself on the boards and on the Senate floor as a player of unique character, conscience, and consistency.

I have had many heroes—political figures and famous people of great achievement, but my true hero has always been my father, William Warren Bradley.

Most people wouldn't realize he was a hero. Even I didn't know how exceptional he was until I reached my twenties. To me, he had just been my dad, a constant source of loving support. Later, I recognized that he was a man of tremendous strength. I believe leaders should be modest and generous and those are the qualities my father personified. He didn't draw attention to himself. He'd always say, "You don't have to be loud to be strong."

My father was a small-town banker in Crystal City, Missouri. His own father died around the time he turned nine. Later he was forced to go to work after just one year of high school. At 16, he started working on the Missouri & Illinois Railroad. At twenty-one, he took a job at the only bank in town, "shining pennies," as he used to say. By the time he was 40, he was the majority shareholder and president of that bank.

He used to say that his proudest accomplishment was that throughout the Great Depression he never foreclosed on a single home. That gives you the mark of the man. He loved lending people money and then seeing that money help them build a house, buy a car, improve their lives. He earned tremendous respect in town for his integrity and for the role he played. Every time I see the movie *It's a Wonderful Life*, I think of him. That's how everyone viewed my father, and I felt especially privileged being his son.

My father suffered from calcified arthritis of the lower spine by the age of forty. I never saw him throw a ball, drive a car, tie his shoes, or walk farther than four or five blocks. But he never complained. Even though he was forced to reassess his entire life, he showed a lot of grace and courage. He demonstrated that over a lifetime, as you age or illness sets in, you have to make adjustments. He showed me that just because your body is diminished, your spirit doesn't have to follow suit. He continued to be active in the community despite his disability. That, to me, is grace.

When I was afraid or unsure, I was completely comfortable sharing my feelings with my father. I could pour out all my fears, and he would reassure me. When I did make mistakes, he never dwelt on them. He trusted me to learn from my mistakes.

My father's physical ailments probably influenced my athleticism. I think his absence of physical ability ironically gave me free reign to develop my own. There was no competition between the father throwing the ball and the son catching it, no father as a giant figure who won every game he played.

When my father did have an agenda or a preference among the choices I made, he operated quietly, behind the scenes. Toward the end of high school, I received 75 basketball scholarship offers. I chose Duke, which had one of the best basketball programs in the country. My mother was delighted. My father didn't question the decision but said, "I think you ought to go to Europe." I'd never been out of the country and neither had he, so this was a great surprise.

So I went to Europe on a tour. As part of the trip, my father suggested I visit Oxford. I did, and I fell in love with the place. When I returned home, I read about something called the Rhodes Scholarship that sent you to Oxford. I read that there were more Rhodes scholars from Princeton University than any other university. The problem was that Princeton hadn't offered me a scholarship because, at that time, and to this day, Princeton remains a nonscholarship school.

A few days before freshman classes convened at Duke, I decided that I'd like to switch to Princeton. I had no idea what the future would hold. In my mind, I was choosing academics over basketball, and it was a tough decision. Only after all this did I realize that my father had always wanted me to go to Princeton. He'd never said so directly; instead, he sent me to Europe so I could find out for myself. He took a chance, but he took a chance because he trusted in me.

In basketball you get to an age when you can no longer play competitively. You're almost certainly looking at retirement by your late forties. The challenge becomes to look at life in a new and different way to make the most of the time you have. You dig deep and find your second wind. That's what my father did, and that's what I've tried to do.

My life turned out very differently from his. He was physically impaired, and I became an athlete. He was a Republican—until Nixon, when he became an independent—and I joined the Democratic Party. He didn't care which party I was in. He supported *me,* whichever party I joined. In giving me room, he expressed confidence that I could handle that room.

My father taught me values that inform my life every day. I think that my gentleness comes from my father. And I also think that my strength comes from him, my perspective. Taking the long view of life, never letting a single defeat end the quest to live fully and honorably, that comes from him.

I think he brought me to a launching point and bade me farewell. He gave me the confidence to believe in myself because he believed in me.

William Warren Bradley died in 1994 and my mother followed in 1995. I went to Crystal City, Missouri, and I went through all the things one has to deal with, and I gave myself a lot of time to cry.

I think the mark of a great father is when he's prepared his son to live in the world when he's not around. And I think that he did that with me. I miss him. Sometimes I'd like to hug him and tell him I love him. But when he went, he knew he'd done his job. I'm a very lucky man.

Bill Bradley

Reverend Doctor Calvin O. Butts, III

*A*t *the center of New York City's Harlem, the nation's lead-*
ing African-American cultural center, is the historic Abyssinian
Baptist Church; and at the center of the Abyssinian Baptist
Church is the Reverend Calvin Otis Butts, III.

From this pivotal position, this committed and outspoken
leader reaches out to thousands of parishioners in Harlem, and
millions more through his radio show. As magnetic and powerful
on the evening news as he is on the pulpit, Butts not only offers
the comfort of religious faith, but the promise of improved race
and community relations to all New Yorkers.

He has courageously stepped forward to address the issues
raised by the spread of HIV/AIDS in the black community and
has served as the president of Africare, an organization dedicated
to improving rural life in Africa. But he is primarily known
for his position on community development and economic self-
determination—and for his own business sense. He has used that
acumen to rejuvenate his underfunded church, and to reinvent a

troubled high school, return a once-bankrupt YMCA to Harlem, and to create $300 million worth of development, including low-income housing for seniors and the homeless. Most recently, he has assumed the position of president of the State University of New York at Old Westbury.

Where once there were burnt-out buildings, drug dealers, and massive unemployment, there is now a thriving community, anchored by black-owned businesses and housing for those who need it. Reverend Calvin Butts deserves much of the credit for Harlem's revitalization, and in so doing, he has ministered not only to its body, but to its soul.

Dr. Benjamin Elijah Mays is my hero. Dr. Mays fought on behalf of young, black men who deserve an opportunity to demonstrate that they are as intelligent, as moral, as brave, and as able to achieve as any other men or persons in this world. He believed in the dignity of *all* human beings, and his life reflected that ideal.

Benjamin Mays was born the eighth child of tenant farmers in a small town in Greenwood County, South Carolina, in 1894. From the very beginning, he had to overcome the poverty and racism that plagued his birthplace. Hard work and intellectual curiosity triumphed, and Benjamin Mays excelled in his every scholarly endeavor. He was valedictorian of his high school class, a Phi Beta Kappa graduate of Bates

College, and he earned a master's degree at the University of Chicago. Later, he became the president of Morehouse College and one of the greatest educators of the twentieth century.

His chief crusade was to rid the world of prejudice for the betterment of all people. He said, "The chief sin of segregation is the distortion of human personality. It damages the soul of both the segregator and segregated."

He was a man who could engage an audience, a powerful orator. He comported himself with distinction and set forth ideas that changed minds. His influence has produced hundreds of medical doctors, Ph.D.s, political leaders, clergy persons, and civil servants who have helped spread his idea of nobility, morality, and character throughout the United States and many parts of the world.

I admired him so much that I aspired to be like him. Today, as a clergyman in one of the most important churches in America, as president of a college, and as a man committed to improving life in New York, I am hopefully attaining some of what Dr. Mays achieved in his lifetime. No other man, with the exception of my father, has had that kind of impact on me.

I first became aware of Dr. Mays as an adolescent, somewhere between ten and thirteen years of age. My mother took me to hear him speak on at least three occasions. I was just a boy, but his speeches made such an impact that I can still remember much of the content. I learned that he was the president of Morehouse College in Atlanta and decided I wanted to go there when it came time to continue my education.

Dr. Mays retired from Morehouse during my freshman year, but he was still very present on the campus as president emeritus. He had earned the school an international reputation for excellence in scholarship, leadership, and service. Students loved to hear him speak. I remember he would often recite a short poem that included the line, "I've got just a minute, but eternity is in it." It was to let you know that when you stood up to speak before an audience, you had to make use of the moment. More importantly, make sure what you say is of value.

This lesson became evident sometime during my freshman year when I was opening an account at a bank in town. The teller who was waiting on me seemed to be taking too long to get the account together. I needed to get back to campus for class, and I became irritated. The longer the teller took, the more impatient I became. I complained and my voice rose. Then from down at the other end of the bank I heard a voice say, "Mr. Butts, that is not appropriate for a Morehouse man!"

I looked up and it was Dr. Mays. He looked at me and said, "Morehouse men do not behave that way."

Well, I straightened up! The experience made me realize a

couple of things: First, what kind of behavior was expected of me as a representative of my learning institution. And second, Dr. Mays knew my name! I was shamed by my behavior but still flattered that this powerful, charismatic man knew my name.

Dr. Mays was in this world, but he wasn't of this world. The bank incident happened almost forty years ago, and I remember it clear as a bell today. When Dr. Mays spoke to you, you remembered what he said.

As I got older, I came to appreciate his bravery and the scope of his work. He was a real revolutionary. He was training black men to be strong, to be leaders, to be intellectually rigorous, and to stand against an oppressive and racist society. And he was doing that in the 1930s and '40s!

Many people don't know that Dr. Mays was once Martin Luther King, Jr.'s, teacher. Martin King studied under Dr. Mays at Morehouse and was greatly influenced by his emphasis on nonviolence as a means of political protest. Dr. Martin Luther King, Jr., considered Mays to be his "spiritual mentor" and "intellectual father." Martin Luther King, Jr., asked us to judge people not by the color of their skin but by the content of their character. He got that kind of thinking from Dr. Mays.

When I have to face challenging situations or I feel a little troubled or insecure, Dr. Mays immediately comes up in my mind. He set the standard for me. I remember his words and his example: "Do not let a situation intimidate you. You've been prepared to meet any challenge."

I think he changed the face of America because he influenced so many Morehouse graduates. The most famous is, of course, Martin Luther King, Jr., but Julian Bond, Lerone Bennett, Otis Moss, and Olatunje Babatunde—one of the great African drummers whose music has inspired millions, not only in Africa but all over the world—are Morehouse graduates. In addition, there are thousands of others who work as civil servants, physicians, scientists, college presidents, and artists all over the country. You may never hear the names of these men, but they are important people who have been providing strong leadership in their local communities. They are also fathers and husbands and friends to countless others. Dr. Mays's sphere of influence is far-reaching and continues to grow.

Ultimately, the world should commend Dr. Mays for the sense of pride and leadership he instilled in Morehouse men, for dealing with very tough racial situations, and for convincing people in the deep south that educating black men was the right thing to do.

When I was a senior at Morehouse, Dr. Mays asked me to do research for his book *Born to Rebel.* My name in the acknowledgments was my first writing credential and it was a great honor. Years later, Dr. Mays was an invited speaker at our church, and I had the pleasure of spending time with him again. Dr. Mays never failed to impress me with his intellectual stamina, his powerful sermons, and his ethical standards. He was an ordained Baptist preacher, a deeply faithful Christian, and a dedicated family man. He was devoted to his students, who, under his leadership, became his family.

Dr. Mays once told a group of students, "I will live in vain if I do not act so that you will be freer than I am—freer intellectually, freer politically, and freer economically." His legacy is proof that he did not live in vain.

Richard "Bo" Dietl

In his sixteen years as one of New York's Finest, Richard "Bo" Dietl made more than 1,500 arrests and became one of the most highly decorated detectives in the history of the New York City Police Department, with more than 80 awards and commendations for bravery. They called him "One Tough Cop." Like many police officers, Dietl does not consider his work on the force to be heroic, but the truth is that these men and women put themselves in harm's way every day to keep us safe, and that's heroic by any standards—especially when they repeatedly go above and beyond the call of duty, as Dietl did.

Someone else might have seen retirement as an invitation to take it easy, but Dietl rededicated himself to the safety of the citizenry. In his current position as the chairman of Beau Dietl & Associates, Dietl controls security for some of the nation's most prominent companies. His concern, in particular, for the safety of our children has led to the development of software that allows parents to monitor their children's contacts on the Internet. The security of our country has never been more critical, but we can all sleep a little more soundly knowing that Bo Dietl is on the job, helping to keep America safe.

The term *hero* makes me nervous. It gets thrown around a lot, sometimes carelessly. I get upset, for example, when that term is used to describe anything I did when I was on the police force. I was just doing my job, and to me that is not heroism.

This also might not be popular to say, but just because someone happens to get killed because they're in the wrong place at the wrong time doesn't automatically make them a hero. On the other hand, people who make the choice to go into combat, knowing that there's mortal danger around every turn, or people who run into burning buildings to help the people inside—those people are heroes in my book. To me being a hero means that you've demonstrated your willingness to make a supreme sacrifice for others—either by literally risking your own life or by dedicating your life to helping others. To me, heroes are people who willingly sacrifice to fight for what they believe in—whether that's the United States of America or the safety and comfort of one child.

My friend Don Imus is a hero. It's true that he conquered alcoholism and drugs to become a top media personality and one of America's most influential people, but that's not the reason he's a hero to me. CEOs of major corporations, and United States senators and representatives vie to get on his show, which has a loyal listening audience of 10 million people—but that's not why he's a hero.

The people who really get Imus's attention are kids with terminal diseases. He built a big ranch out in New Mexico so he'd have some place to invite these kids to have a holiday, and it's an experience that they often describe as the best time of their lives. They're not babied at the ranch; they ride horses and do chores, mucking out the stalls and feeding the animals, like they would if they weren't sick. Sometimes, it's the first time that they've been able to do things without someone worrying about them, whether that's their parents or the staff at a hospital. Imus makes them feel normal, just by hanging out with them. He doesn't feel sorry for them because he doesn't want them to feel sorry for themselves.

It takes a lot of strength to do what he does, to create bonds with kids who probably aren't going to make it. But he does it over and over again. He doesn't need to do it—he doesn't need the publicity, that's for sure—but he's dedicated his life to taking care of and helping these children.

What makes him a hero for me isn't just what he does with those kids, but the fact that he raises awareness about them. On his show he's always talking about issues like autism and children living with disabilities. Because of him, I've come to recognize and to appreciate an entire category of real, every-day heroes: all parents of children with severe disabilities or autism.

Parenting such a child is a full-time job, 24 hours a day, seven days a week. There's no coffee break, and it doesn't change on Thanksgiving or Christmas. These parents have to be constantly vigilant, constantly alert. As they get older, they have to worry about what's going to happen to their children when they're gone. As great as the sacrifice is, there's no recognition in it. For every family on the Movie of the Week, there are thousands, maybe millions, of parents just struggling to get through day to day.

Those parents are heroes, because they've given their lives for someone else, putting their own needs second every time.

Dr. Felton Earls

*O*n *April 5, 1968, the neurophysiologist Dr. Felton Earls emerged from a soundproof room in an underground laboratory at the University of Wisconsin, where he had spent the last 36 hours mapping the responses of a cat's brain to high- and low-frequency sounds. What he found was a campus in an uproar, and a totally changed world; Dr. Martin Luther King had been assassinated.*

At that moment, Earls decided he could not in good conscience spend his career shut off in the cloister of the academic laboratory. He rededicated himself immediately to what he calls society's best hope: our children, and the communities that nurture them. He switched professional gears to gain degrees as a pediatrician, a child psychiatrist, and a professor of human behavior and development at the Harvard School of Public Health.

Earls has become a social scientist in the most literal sense of the term—a doctor who treats communities. According to a Jan-

uary 6, 2004, article in the New York Times *called "On Crime as Science (One Neighbor at a Time)," his groundbreaking field research is credited with debunking the "broken windows" theory of crime and is turning the field of criminology on its head. His research reveals a startling finding: The most important determinant with respect to crime rates is not race, IQ, family, or individual temperament, but the willingness of neighbors to act, when needed, for one another's benefit, particularly for the benefit of one another's children.*

The policy implications of his work are far-reaching. In the words of a former director of the National Institute of Justice, this finding is "far and away the most important research insight in the last decade."

Earls is currently collaborating with his wife of 32 years, the neurophysiologist Mary Carlson, M.D., on a project to promote the well-being of the devastating number of children who have been orphaned by AIDS in Tanzania.

My hero is Charles Darwin, the nineteenth-century naturalist. This long-dead white Englishman may seem a strange choice: after all, Martin Luther King, Jr., changed the course of my life. And as a child, I desperately wanted to be a musician, so why not one of the many jazz artists who continue to enrich and enliven my life, like Louis Armstrong (my homeboy from New Orleans), Miles Davis, Keith Jarrett, or John

Coltrane? I could stretch it and claim one of these men as well, but I don't need two heroes; I need only one.

No one has had as great an influence on me—as a scientist, or a man—as Charles Darwin. His scientific rigor, intellectual brilliance, and the innovative nature of his methods have influenced, challenged, and comforted me countless times. So many aspects of his life and work directly touch my own that I consider myself to be permanently in his grasp.

I was probably about sixteen or seventeen years old when I first read *Voyage of the Beagle,* and I devoured every page with a sense of astonishment. How could anyone compile such detailed notes and weigh the evidence stemming from so many ideas all at the same time?

As impressed as I was by the comprehensiveness, the thing that had the most profound effect on me was Darwin's method. Up until that point, I had thought of science as something that took place in a laboratory: you harvested specimens from their natural environment, brought them back to an artificial space, and controlled everything about them as you observed them.

What Darwin did in the South Seas was the exact opposite. He was, first and foremost, an ecologist, dedicated to understanding things *in their place.* The world itself, in its natural form, was his laboratory, and his work was a vital and dynamic part of the natural world—not apart from it. The idea that you could do fundamentally important science outside of the managed environment of the laboratory was revolutionary to me, and it had a direct impact on the methods I chose to adopt in my own work and continue to use today.

As I was to learn firsthand, it's not always easy to work without the conventional apparatus of a laboratory. You're viewed as an outsider, and there still is a pervasive idea that research done this way is somehow less scientific or rigorous than work done in the lab. It has comforted me, over the years, to know that this method resulted in Darwin's theory of evolution, one of the single most significant achievements in science. But I have taken another cue from Darwin, who answered critics of his method by bringing the rigor of the laboratory to the field.

To my mind, he is the consummate scientist, the exemplary standard, and he sets the bar for me every time I design an experiment or an instrument to analyze data. Darwin painstakingly collected his own data, analyzed it with attention to infinite number of details, and then patiently interpreted his findings in the most elegant and groundbreaking way possible. The controversy about his work always strikes me as ironic, because he was such a conservative scientist. He was so meticulous that his methods would stand up to a National Institutes of Health review board today.

Another, often overlooked, aspect of Darwin's work was his social sensitivity. He was a devoutly religious person; in fact, it was while studying to be a cleric that he seized an opportunity to travel the South Seas as naturalist on board the *Beagle*. And although he was initially reluctant to bring humans into his grand theory—*The Origin of Species* is pretty much exclusively about the lower orders of animal life—the miserable social conditions he witnessed on his voyages do not escape his notice. For example, in the final pages of *Voyage of the Beagle*, he criticizes the institution of slavery: "On the 19th of August we finally left the shores of Brazil. I thank God, I shall never again visit a slave-country. To this day, if I hear a distant scream, it recalls with painful vividness my feelings, when passing a house near, I heard the pitiable moans, and could not but suspect that some poor slave was being tormented, yet knew that I was as powerless as a child to remonstrate."

This sensitivity to the human condition was always at the root of the way Darwin pondered life on Earth, and that concern is boldly outlined in the later two books he wrote on human development. In those books, he links the biology of life with the morality of man.

This connection captured my consciousness totally, and eventually formed the basis for one of the biggest ethical decisions I have made over the course of my life: the decision to become a conscientious objector when I was drafted to fight in the war in Vietnam.

I had already been persuaded by Martin Luther King, Jr.,

that nonviolence was a stronger force than retaliation, a hard lesson to learn. But as important as Dr. King's moral leadership and spirit were to me, it was Darwin, ultimately, who helped me to focus my thoughts about war.

Darwin believed that humans were part of the natural order, and his writing instilled in me a terrific respect for our place in that order. Furthermore, he proposed the idea that humans are a fundamentally social species; we have evolved in a way to make us respond to others in a sympathetic way. He believed that we are designed to recognize and protest injustice, even as very young children, because a social species survives best when its members take care of one another. This conclusion moved me deeply, and I believed that war was the most horrible contradiction of those principles imaginable. It was a contradiction in which I could not, and would not, participate.

Darwin—the man and his methods—continues to inspire and guide me today. One thing in particular gives me hope for my own future. Although Darwin took long trips away from home, he also spent long periods of time in seclusion with his family at Down House, his home and garden in the south of England, assimilating what he'd learned. Once he had all the data he needed, he turned away from the scrutiny of his peers to master his understanding of living things.

The feeling of his separateness from the academy was the

thing that stood out for me when I visited his house thirty years ago—and at this stage in my life, it is the part of his method I most wish to emulate. I admire the fact that he used his aloofness (whether the result of an actual illness, or hypochondriasis, the diagnosis that the psychiatrist in me finds most satisfying) to create a space to reflect.

I am a social scientist and a child psychiatrist, with interest in violence, morality, democracy, and global justice—interests that cannot be contained by the narrow confines of institutional life. I very much want to embark upon a free and creative exploration of the world in which I live and which I care deeply about. But as an institutionalized scientist, my time is spent in attending committees; in organizing and supervising a team of research assistants, statisticians, and administrators to execute field work; and in data analysis and publication. I spend far too much of my time teaching, writing grants, and pondering budgets, rather than thinking and writing.

I have been on a voyage for much of my life, one that has taken me all over the world in search of solutions to enhancing the well-being of children. Like my hero, I still aspire to spend some years putting my ideas, insights, and small discoveries in order. In desperate moments I wonder if I should model Darwin and feign sickness—or contract malaria on my next trip to Africa! But heroes are not to be imitated; they are to be admired.

In this way (as in countless others over the last fifty years), Darwin's example extends to me a beacon of hope and optimism that I might also have a few years to reflect upon what I have learned.

Kathy Eldon

On July 12, 1993, Reuters photographer Dan Eldon and three of his colleagues heard that U.N. forces had bombed the safe house of a Somali warlord. The warlord was not in residence, but 74 innocent men, women, and children were killed in the blast, with many more injured. As the journalists began to document the atrocity on behalf of those wrongly killed, an enraged and grief-stricken mob surrounded and attacked them. All four journalists were stoned to death.

Dan Eldon's mother, Kathy Eldon, is a writer, journalist, and television and film producer. With compassion, forgiveness, and grace, she has turned the loss of her son—arguably the most terrible personal tragedy a mother can endure—into an affirmation of life itself. Dubbed "Leharo," or "the one who laughs," by a Masai woman whose family he befriended, Dan's short life was dedicated to travel, art, and the spirit of giving. His mother shared that passion with the world when she took his art- and word-filled journal pages, and collected them in a volume called

The Journey Is the Destination. *She is also the author of a number of best-selling guided journals, including* Soul Catcher, Angel Catcher, *and* Love Catcher.

Kathy is the founder of Creative Visions, a television and film production company, and much of her work, including an Emmy-nominated Turner Broadcasting film on frontline journalists, Dying to Tell the Story, *has to do with issues of journalistic freedom and safety. She is currently developing a film about her son. She and her daughter Amy also cofounded the Creative Visions Foundation, which offers grants to young people who wish to produce projects with a social, humanitarian, or environmental focus, and the DEPOT, the Dan Eldon Place of Tomorrow, a youth center to help young people achieve their potential, based in Nairobi.*

I have always believed that we have a lot to learn from young people. My two children, Dan and Amy Eldon, have been two of my greatest teachers—and heroes.

Half Jewish-Rumanian, like their father, Mike, and half Protestant-American, like me, they were born in England, though when they were very young, our family moved to Kenya where I decided to try my wings as a journalist. Determined to tell stories about the extraordinary accomplishments of ordinary people, I brought home many of my subjects—everyday heroes like Father Groll, a laconic Dutch missionary who offered hope to the poorest of the poor; Nairobi street kids, prostitutes, and slum-dwellers; John and Joan Karmali, who started the country's first multiracial school; and Kenyan cameraman Mohamed Amin, whose courageous coverage of the 1982 Ethiopian famine ignited a global response that led to Bob Geldof's *Live Aid* concert.

I watched with pride as Dan and Amy began to emulate those they admired. At twelve, Dan helped a destitute Masai family by selling their intricately beaded jewelry to his teachers, friends, and tourists, hitching a ride to his African "mother" to hand over the profits. At fifteen, he launched a "Save a Heart" appeal to pay for an operation for an impoverished Kenyan child. Determined to fund-raise quickly, he and Amy turned our backyard into a nightclub, charging friends to attend noisy benefit rock concerts. As a freshman at Pasadena Community College, Dan founded Student Transport Aid to help survivors of a cruel civil war raging in Mozambique. Dan and the STA team, including 15-year-old Amy, raised $17,000, and delivered the aid in person to a refugee camp. The expedition changed the lives of every student on the trip.

When Dan was twenty-one and working as Reuters' youngest correspondent, he traveled to Somalia to cover a little-known famine threatening the lives of millions. Like those of his hero Mohamed Amin, Dan's photos were among the first to awaken the world's conscience and led to a multinational relief mission, "Operation Restore Hope." Dan, a true "son of Africa," returned to Somalia many times in the next year, reporting on the decline of the country into anarchy. The American-led mission turned into a disastrous situation for all involved, as dissident Somalis raided aid convoys and killed UN Peacekeepers. In retaliation, on July 12, 1993, UN troops in Blackhawk helicopters attacked a villa where they believed the principal warlord, self-styled "General" Aideed, was hiding. Unfortunately, he wasn't there and during the ill-advised bombing, more than 200 innocent people were killed or wounded.

Rushed to the scene by survivors, Dan and three colleagues began photographing the carnage, only to be stoned to death by a mob enraged by the deaths of their loved ones. Upon hearing the news I was utterly devastated, lost myself in a blur of grief and pain. Just when I might have given up, my amazing daughter Amy brought me back to life. Enrolling at Boston University's College of Communications, she decided to follow in her brother's footsteps, not as a war correspondent, but as a "peace correspondent," telling stories that would bring people together, not tear them apart. Amy's commitment to her purpose helped me find mine. I realized that I could never regain what I've lost, but Dan's spirit of compassion could guide my path to the future. Focused on transforming my anger into a positive force, I worked with Amy to develop *Dying to Tell the Story,* a film about journalists at risk, in which she interviewed top frontline correspondents including CNN's Christiane Amanpour, BBC anchor Martin Bell, and British photographer Don McCullen. As proud mom and executive producer, I was thrilled when our film premiered at the United Nations and CNN aired it in 200 countries.

Inspired by the response, we produced other films, including GlobalTribe, a PBS series about everyday heroes seeking solutions to global issues. We have been overwhelmed by the response of viewers who have written to ask how they could get involved. Today Amy and a team of talented young producers have developed the GlobalTribe Network (globaltribenet.org), an exciting Internet-based resource that gives young people the inspiration, tools, and resources they need to make a difference in their local and our global community. Providing a hub of intelligence and creative tools, the project taps into the limitless potential of youth, and encourages them to—in the words of my greatest hero, Mahatma Gandhi—"be the change" we wish to see in the world.

In the years since Dan's death I have found it possible to transform my hurt and anger into a sense of gratitude for my son's short but remarkable life, and for his ongoing inspiration to others. Fueled by his powerful energy and by Amy's gentle spirit, I have found my true purpose: to use the power of the media to share the stories of everyday heroes, each of whom becomes a part of our GlobalTribe, an ever-expanding network of change makers that extends across the planet—and beyond.

My children have been a source of true inspiration and have taught me firsthand the wisdom of Winston Churchill's quotation: "Making a living is what you get. Making a life is what you give."

Kathy Eldon

Michael J. Fox

*A*s *an actor, Michael J. Fox defined the eighties for us on both the big and little screens; first, as Alex P. Keaton, the endearing and enthusiastic Republican son on television's* Family Ties, *and second, in* Back to the Future *as young Marty McFly in the time-travel blockbuster trilogy. His legions of fans were understandably elated to have him back in 1995 as Michael Flaherty in the smash hit* Spin City.

What his fans didn't know was that Fox had been diagnosed with Parkinson's disease in 1991. Dreading sensationalistic publicity, he decided with his family and his doctors that they would keep the diagnosis under wraps. Seven years after the diagnosis, Fox decided it was time to announce his disease to the public in a move that would have radical implications not only for his own life, but for the future for all people suffering with Parkinson's.

In response to that announcement came a tidal outpouring of empathy and concern from the public, and Michael J. Fox knew he had the opportunity to turn his personal battle into a global fight on behalf of every person who suffers from degenerative neurological disorders. With his wife, Tracy Pollan, Michael established the Michael J. Fox Foundation for Parkinson's Research. This foundation has become the largest not-for-profit funder of Parkinson's disease research.

Fox's courage in coming forward, combined with his charm, humility, and natural optimism, have succeeded in moving the frontiers of science and raised awareness about Parkinson's exponentially. He knows there is a cure within reach and is committed to doing whatever it takes to get us there.

I think that a lot of times people think of heroes as larger-than-life individuals who do the extraordinary. I'm like everybody else in that respect and my larger-than-life heroes are the same as a lot of people's—Martin Luther King, Jr.; Mohandas K. Gandhi; and Rosa Parks.

Muhammad Ali is another great hero of mine. He is an imperfect man, but he has taken powerful stands in the most basic human way and with such dignity. When I finally met and spoke with him, it was tremendously humbling.

But in addition to those heroes who act on a grand scale, there is another breed—the everyday heroes. They serve as a moral compass, pointing the way to right thinking and right action in our daily lives.

My older brother Steve is one of these heroes for me. He and his wife Laureen did nothing more than raise a son who was born with spinal bifida—but raised him with such patience and love and commitment, without self-pity or a sense of martyrdom. They just loved their son and raised him.

Those are the same values my parents had. Now that I'm a parent, they are even greater heroes to me. They raised five kids on a military salary, moved all across Canada, and still managed to create a strong family bond that endures to this day. My wife, Tracy, and I are raising four kids with far more resources, luxuries, and time, and I hope that we do as good a job.

And then there's Debi Brooks, the president and CEO of our foundation. When I started the Michael J. Fox Foundation for Parkinson's Research, I thought we needed someone with a personal connection to the disease. So the first question I asked Debi was, "Do you know anyone with Parkinson's?" I was surprised to learn that Debi had no direct experience of this disease, nor any family member or close friend afflicted, which is often the spur that leads someone to get personally involved. This is one of the things that I find most remarkable about Debi. It is rare to find someone who can commit as strongly and as passionately as she does without having that sort of personal interest in the cause.

Debi has taken on this fight as though her own life and the lives of those closest to her were on the line. She's also got what it takes to back up those good intentions. A brilliant operational and strategic planner, she knows how to marshal ideas and people toward a common goal.

The decision to work with us to cure Parkinson's has required sacrifice, both personally and financially. The skills, dedication, heart, and integrity she brings to the Foundation would guarantee her wild success wherever she applied herself—but Debi looked beyond those traditional trappings. She is always going full throttle and it has nothing to do with applause or being in the spotlight or getting credit—for her it is all about getting the job done.

In a very real way, Debi is fighting my fight and I couldn't ask for a better champion and partner to stand up to Parkinson's. She is truly a force of nature and I often joke that we are fortunate that she chooses to use her powers for good.

All my heroes—Debi, my brother, and my parents, Ali, and the rest—have become a personal reference library of instinct and actions. Very often I ask myself in the immediate sense, "How would Steve or my father look at this?" Or in the bigger sense, "How would Gandhi deal with this?" So if there is a common trait among all my heroes it is this: They are all people who become extraordinary by virtue of their willingness to stand up and fight for the right thing: fight for freedom; for justice and equality; fight against disease or against the odds to keep their families whole and safe. What could be more heroic than that?

Frank O. Gehry

Frank Gehry, one of the most celebrated of living architects, resides in Southern California and works throughout the world. He has designed fantastically original, award-winning buildings, ranging from family homes to concert halls and museums. His major public buildings—including the Guggenheim Museum in Bilbao, Spain; the Walt Disney Concert Hall in Los Angeles; and the Experience Music Project in Seattle—are some of the most inspirational and forward-looking edifices of our times.

Gehry's ingenious designs successfully combine imaginative and practical concerns, in which the commonplace materials of everyday life and the industrial world are used to produce extraordinary results. Each of his buildings is beautifully sited, connecting new structures to the existing environment in a well-considered yet completely new way, with the result that the buildings belong as much to the landscape and the city streets that surround them as they do to the people who work or live within their walls.

I've had many heroes in my life. I was very poor in my early years, and everything seemed beyond my reach.

When I was in high school, I wasn't interested in architecture at all. I was interested in science and electronics, and that was what I read. I used to go every Friday night to a lecture series at the University of Toronto, where they'd perform experiments onstage. I went by myself, mostly because I could never get any of my friends to go with me.

I remember one lecture in particular, when I was sixteen years old. It was given by this white-haired gentleman with a bentwood chair. Actually, I don't remember much about the lecture at all, but I do remember the chair, which affected me as deeply as any piece of art I'd ever seen. I couldn't get it out of my mind. It was beautiful, but that wasn't all. It had a humanistic quality, a respect for human feeling, that made a real impact on me at the time and for years to come. It was an impact I wouldn't fully understand until later.

I didn't know what I wanted to be, so I went to work as a truck driver and took night classes in art at the University of Southern California. I loved ceramics—although I didn't do very well in those courses—because I loved the glazes; I was fascinated with the science of how they're made. Glen Lukens was my ceramics teacher there. He'd cracked the formula for a Chinese blue glaze, and was helping to create a ceramics industry for poor people in Haiti.

Glen changed the course of my life. He was building a house with the architect Raphael Soriano, and he had a feeling that I might like to see the process, so he dragged me over there one day. Soriano was there, wearing an all-black outfit with a black beret, giving directions in his accented English (he was from the Isle of Rhodes), and telling men how to put up steel. I really got into it.

The next day, Glen called me into his office. He said, "You know, I have this hunch. Will you go along with me?" I said, "Whatever you say, boss." He signed me up (and paid for) a night school architecture class. That class was the first time I did something that got people saying, "Hey, there's something going on here." They liked what I did and I enjoyed it, and the school skipped me into the second year.

There, an odd thing happened. I learned about the legendary Finnish architect Alvar Aalto's work, and suddenly, I remembered seeing *that* chair. I thought "Oh, my God, that must be the guy!" Aalto's work had the same profound effect on me as it had had when I was a teenager. I've always thought that architecture should be something that people want to be in. It should be new, not a repetition of the past, and it should have feeling. Aalto was able to do that.

I went to Finland for the first time in 1972 to see all of Aalto's buildings, and I ended up at his studio. He wasn't there, but they let me sit in his chair, so I stayed there for an hour and drank in his world. As I was leaving, I asked his assistant if she could check the archives, to see if he had been the speaker at the University of Toronto in November 1946. Sure enough, it was right there in his records.

So perhaps you could say that I have two heroes, Alvar Aalto and Glen Lukens. One indirectly put me in touch with the other. They certainly worked together in a way to make me the person and the architect I am today.

Mayor Rudolph Giuliani

At the moment of America's greatest crisis, one man took the reins and led a bewildered and frightened people through their darkest hour. This two-term mayor of New York City made his entrance on the global stage on September 11, 2001, when his heroic leadership gave comfort, strength, and solace to a frightened city, nation, and world. Often it is under the most extreme circumstances that our true mettle is tested, and under fire this mayor shown so brightly that his leadership became a beacon around the globe. In a tribute to that display of extraordinary leadership during America's darkest hour, Newsweek *magazine said, "Mayor Giuliani is our Winston Churchill, walking the rubble, calming and inspiring his heartbroken but defiant people."*

Ronald Reagan exemplified a principle that I think defines a great leader. He knew what he believed. Ronald Reagan developed his core beliefs over years of experience leading the Screen Actors Guild and traveling the country giving talks on behalf of General Electric Company. He was clear in communicating those beliefs and he stuck to the same principles whether they were popular or unpopular.

Ronald Reagan was deeply loyal to his core set of values. I followed his career from the 1960s on, and throughout, he held the same views on the need to restrain the size of government, the same views on the value of the private sector, the same views on tax reductions as a way of stimulating the economy, the same views on the need for a strong national defense, and the same views on the dangers of communism. When Ronald Reagan was elected president in 1980, he was able to enact dramatic changes because he had campaigned honestly about who he was and what he believed. He got elected for who he was, not for who he pretended to be. When he then did exactly what he promised, even those who disagreed with his beliefs knew where he stood and appreciated his character.

For example, Reagan believed that communism was an evil that had to be combated and confronted. In large part because of the relentless pressure that Reagan brought to bear, the Soviet Union lost its iron grip much faster. Hundreds of millions of people live in a safer, freer world because of Ronald Reagan's refusal to accept the notion that communism had to be tolerated and appeased.

In addition to developing a set of beliefs, Ronald Reagan exemplified many other characteristics of a leader. He was loyal to his employees, which gave them the confidence to undertake bold initiatives. He was a legendary communicator: he let people know not just what he planned to do, but why he planned to do it. He was also funny and warm, and exuded confidence. I got to see some of these qualities firsthand, because I had the privilege of serving as Associate Attorney General for Ronald Reagan from 1981 to 1983. I was also privileged to be appointed by him as United States Attorney for the Southern District of New York. Ronald Reagan is my hero for all of these reasons and more, and he deserves to be a hero to all who love freedom.

Senator John Glenn

In 1962, at the height of the Cold War, when the USA and the USSR were pitted against each other, John Glenn was launched into space, the first American to orbit the earth. The Berlin Wall had just been erected, and the previous year saw two Russian cosmonauts successfully orbit the earth, propelling the Russians to the head of the space race. Americans needed a patriotic boost, and NASA's success did just that, with Glenn as the icon of a renewed American pride.

Perhaps John Glenn will be most remembered as the hero in a space suit, but he was a strong and honorable figure long before his fame as an astronaut. Growing up in a small town, John learned about the values of hard work, civic duty, and patriotism. Glenn's affinity for flying also began in this small town, with short flights in his father's barnstormer. After the attack on Pearl Harbor, John quit school and enlisted in the Army Air Corps.

A veteran of two wars, Glenn flew more than a hundred com-

bat missions. His military experience put him on the path to a career in aviation, but his sense of honor, hardworking nature, and quick thinking earned him a spot on NASA's first list of astronauts.

In between space missions, Glenn ran for the U.S. Senate, and after a few lost races, was elected senator from Ohio by an overwhelming majority. Senator Glenn fought to clean up decades of environmental waste left by the nuclear weapons surge during the Cold War. After 24 years of service, John retired from the Senate and spent a few years traveling with Annie, his wife of 62 years. Yet, there are times when he wishes he were still working on Capitol Hill.

Glenn's support for the U.S. space program has been unwavering and so has his commitment to education and community service. On the twenty-fifth anniversary of the flight of Friendship 7, Glenn remarked, "The exploration of the unknown is nothing less than an expression of America's spirit." Glenn's outerspace exploration came full circle in 1998, when he completed one last mission on the space shuttle Discovery.

I don't remember when I first met my wife, Annie. Our parents were good friends and we practically grew up in the same playpen. We never knew a time when we didn't know each other. But somewhere in my teens, I took a second look at Annie and liked what I saw.

She has always had a great sense of humor; she was a straight-A student and a wonderful musician. She won a scholarship to Juilliard, but instead she stayed in Ohio, at Muskingum College, and married me. I admired Annie. She was a very talented person, a true standout. Yet, she had this great difficulty.

Annie was a stutterer. She'd have a hang-up on 85 percent of the words she tried to speak, which was a severe handicap. When we were growing up, I knew Annie for the type of person she was, and all the things you'd be attracted to in a person, except for the stuttering. Through the 62 years we have been married and our childhood together, I have seen her reach out so many times. We can just about guess what the other is thinking, but not everybody saw Annie the way I did; they couldn't get beyond the stuttering to know her for all her talents. In school she never tried out for school plays and was never asked to recite. As Annie got older, everyday tasks and conversations were extremely difficult for her, but she did them with great courage.

For Annie, stuttering meant not being able to take a taxi because she would have to write out the address and give it to the driver because she couldn't get the words out. It would be too embarrassing to try to say where she wanted to go. Going to the store is a tremendously difficult and frustrating experience when you can't find what you want and can't ask the clerk because you are too embarrassed about your stutter.

The telephone is another devil for a stutterer. Most stutterers just won't call anybody. Annie couldn't just pick up the phone and call a friend to chat, or even 911. I was in the Marine Corps and was overseas while Annie was at home with our two young children. When I went away, we always made sure that there was a neighbor available in case there was an emergency since Annie would probably not be able to use the telephone.

When I was in Guam, Annie brought our two young children out there to visit. She flew on commercial airlines until she got to San Francisco. Traveling across the country with two children in tow is a great difficulty for anyone, but especially for someone with her kind of communication problem. I saw Annie's perseverance and strength through the years and it just made me admire her and love her even more. It takes guts to operate with a disability; I don't know if I would have had the courage to do all the things that Annie did so well.

When Annie was younger, stutterers were generally assumed to have a psychological problem. Therapy based on that theory helped a few people, but it didn't work with Annie. She had been through every type of treatment there was, and they were of very little help to her. It was a tremendous disappointment because she wanted so much to speak normally. Every time she went through a treatment program or worked with a speech therapist, it didn't work; with consistent disappointments, she despaired of trying again.

Finally, about 20 years ago, we were watching the *Today* show, and a professor, Ron Webster, was talking about the success of his new theory and treatment for stuttering. I turned to Annie, and said, "You should try this because it's brand new." She agreed, and went down to Webster's three-week course in Roanoke, Virginia. It literally changed her life.

In her first week, she learned how to speak in slow, short syllables. During the second week, they gradually sped up the rate at which she spoke, working on sounds that are particularly difficult for stutterers. The third week was a continuation of the work learned in the first two weeks. Annie reached a point where she could represent me in speeches, and speak for others with handicaps. She will always have to work on her speech, but with her courage and determination she overcomes the disability every day with phone calls and normal conversation.

Annie inspired a lot of people to get treatment for their disabilities. Through the American Speech and Hearing Association (ASHA), she would meet with people to tell her story and how she stuck with her treatment. ASHA was impressed enough by Annie's accomplishments that they now give an award in her name. The "Annie" honors people who overcome great communication difficulties and achieve distinction by helping others. Each year we try to make it to the award ceremony, and Annie presents the award. One year, Annie presented the award to James Earl Jones. You would never guess that he was a stutterer by watching him in movie roles, but he, too, has learned to overcome his handicap.

Along with others like Jones, the recipients of the "Annie" exemplify the very definition of the word *hero.* They not only demonstrate tremendous personal strength, but they also choose to use that strength to benefit other people. Despite great difficulties and daily struggles, these individuals don't expect anybody else to take care of them. We tend to think of heroes as being those who are well known, but America is made up of a whole nation of heroes who face problems that are very difficult, and their courage remains largely unsung. Millions of individuals are heroes in their own right. In my book, Annie is one of those heroes.

John Glenn

Erin Gruwell

Erin Gruwell walked into her first year of teaching high school in a racially divided urban community in Southern California to find herself assigned to a classroom of "unteachables," students nobody thought could learn or succeed.

This fiercely determined teacher proved the education system wrong by developing an innovative curriculum that taught tolerance through literature and writing. Her students documented their own struggles with poverty and discrimination, and came to call themselves the Freedom Writers, in a nod to the Freedom Riders who fought segregation in the civil rights era. The project's success is legendary; not only did every single one of those "unteachables" graduate from high school, but many of them are now teaching at some of the country's toughest schools.

Erin Gruwell believes there should be no such thing as "unteachable" children in America. Through scholarships, teacher training workshops, and other programs sponsored by the Erin Gruwell Education Project, one teacher is doing her best to bring

at-risk and economically disadvantaged kids one step closer to
the educations they deserve.

When I first read Anne Frank's *Diary of a Young Girl,* I was living in a suburban home with a manicured lawn in a gated
community, sheltered from the outside world. It was an eye-
opening experience for me. Up to that point in my life, the
heroes in my books rode in on white horses, and the good guy
always won in the end. But in this book, there was no happy
ending; instead, the young hero dies in a concentration camp.

I was overwhelmed with grief and anger at the injustice
and intolerance that had led to Anne Frank's death, but her
honesty and the very existence of the book gave me hope,
too. It was the first time I really understood the power of
words: Anne Frank's words lived on, and they had the power
to change lives.

We owe the existence of the book to Miep Gies, the
tremendously courageous and just woman who helped Anne
Frank and her family hide from the Nazis. Gies not only
risked her own life to provide the Franks with food and supplies, but she found, saved, and eventually shared Anne's
diary.

In 1994, I began teaching high school in Long Beach, California. As a rookie teacher, I was given a class of unteachables, students that no other teacher wanted. Many of my

students had grown up in an environment of violence, racial discrimination, and hate; many of them had participated in the Rodney King riots. They weren't expected to survive, much less graduate. *The Diary of a Young Girl* was one of the tools I used to convey to my students the tremendous power of words. They could then use this power to express their feelings of anger, alienation, and fear, because words were far more powerful than any spray-paint can or Molotov cocktail.

There were some obstacles to overcome. My students weren't issued books at school because the administration thought they'd destroy them. I used my Christmas funds to buy each one of my 150 students a copy of Anne Frank's diary, and I think that simply having books of their own had a profound effect.

I was shocked to discover that many of my students had never heard of the Holocaust at all. So I looked for a way to make history come alive. Since there was no funding for a field trip, I worked two other jobs, moonlighting as a concierge and selling lingerie, so that I could save up enough to take them to the Museum of Tolerance in L.A. The field trip, and the realization that learning isn't just something that happens in a classroom, also had a profound effect on all of us.

Pain transcends geography and time, and my students began to identify with Anne, who was their age. They began to realize that they were themselves living through what they began to call "an undeclared war." The streets of Long

Beach weren't the streets of Europe during World War II, but like Anne Frank, my students had also been discriminated against, and too often found themselves losing friends and loved ones to violence.

Anne also had been surrounded by terrible violence, but she fought back with words instead of weapons. Through her example, my students began to understand that words endure, and can bring about change. They started to write their own diaries, which was a cathartic and liberating experience, but also a terrifying one: when they put something on paper, they made it real.

When we learned that Miep Gies was still alive, we decided to send her our stories and ask her to come visit our class. She came, and became a living bridge between the black-and-white pages of Anne's diary and our own memories and imaginations. She brought to life the reality of what had actually happened in that attic, and she urged my students to "respect Anne's wish that we go on living, to make sure Anne's death was not in vain."

Meeting Miep had a radical effect on my students. She is incredibly humble and gracious, and always deflects any kind of attention by saying, "This is bigger than me," but the fact remains that she put her life on the line. She didn't have to do what she did. There weren't television crews watching, or a book deal to be made. She was saving humanity, and in saving humanity, she was preserving hope for all of us. Before she was captured, Anne Frank wrote, "In spite of everything, I still believe that people are really good at heart." I believe that she had Miep in mind when she wrote those words.

During Miep's lecture to our class, one student who had been particularly inspired by her story stood up and told her that she was his hero. She got very upset and said, "I'm not a hero; I simply did what I had to do, because it was the right thing to do." That became a mantra, for me and for my students. What better guiding principle can you have for making choices than simply to do the right thing?

It has been ten years since my students and I read *The Diary of a Young Girl* together, and met our hero, Miep Gies. The students' stories have been published and the proceeds have been used to help the authors go to college. Today, some of the Freedom Writers are teachers, social workers, doctors, and lawyers. They have spoken on television and before Congress.

It's most exciting for me when we go to speak at schools, and I see my kids challenging a whole new generation of teenagers to put their personal stories onto the page. Through Anne Frank's legacy and the work of Miep Gies, my students and I have truly learned the power of words to change the world.

Scott Hamilton

The champion figure skater Scott Hamilton has proven, over and over again, that there is no challenge too big to overcome.

This 1984 Olympic gold medalist spent the first part of his childhood battling an unknown disease that made him temporarily stop growing at the age of two. Hamilton had never been on the ice at that point, and the activity was suggested simply as something to do now that he was home and healthy, to make him feel like a normal kid again. Fast, confident, and talented, Hamilton turned his small size into an asset, and won numerous national and world titles as well as an Olympic gold medal. He has been inducted into both the Olympic Hall of Fame and the World Figure Skating Hall of Fame.

In 1997, Hamilton was diagnosed with testicular cancer. He fought the disease, and became an inspiration to a whole new audience of people when he founded the Scott Hamilton CARES Initiative, an educational web site that helps cancer patients better understand their disease and treatment. But there were more challenges still to come: in 2004, Hamilton was diagnosed with a brain tumor, which may provide some answers to the illness he suffered as a child.

As illustrious as his career on the ice may have been, his fans most admire his optimism, courage, and fortitude as he faces down his medical challenges with the same exemplary grace and boldness he displayed on the ice.

I've met six presidents, royal families, and industry leaders, but not one of them measures up to the standards of courage, strength, and integrity that my mother, Dorothy Hamilton, possessed. She continues to guide and inspire me, in everything I have accomplished in my skating career, throughout all my health problems, and in my life as a father and husband.

The optimism, energy, and enthusiasm my mother maintained throughout her life, especially in devastating circumstances, was amazing. She didn't need to recite old clichés and parental words of wisdom to inspire us. She led by example, her actions exemplifying the values she intended to instill. She never had to say, "When life hands you lemons, make lemonade." She showed us by living it.

Her life was filled with challenges. When she and my father were starting their family, she had several miscarriages, and lost two babies at birth. She gave birth to twins, but only my older sister survived, and her second baby died just a few hours after he was born. Even with these losses, she didn't retreat into a shell or feel sorry for herself. Instead she announced to my father, "We are going to move ahead. We are going to take a bad situation and make it better, by doing what we always wanted to do. We are going to have a family." They adopted me, and then a few years later, adopted my brother. In a family portrait, we look like total strangers, but Mom tied us all together.

I was very close to my mother, in part because of the unbreakable bond that we formed when I was very young, going in and out of hospitals with an undiagnosable illness. Although she did have to work to support the family, she took as much time away as she could to be with me. She'd either sleep in a chair in my room, or commute back and forth between the hospital and home. She drove back and forth to hospitals in Ann Arbor, Michigan, and Toledo, Ohio, and went up to the children's hospital in Boston to meet with the specialist there. She must have been exhausted, but she never showed it; she was always focused on helping me to forget that I was living in a sterile environment, away from home, with doctors sticking needles in me all the time. From my perspective as a child, it looked effortless, but now I know how difficult it must have been. She made great sacrifices to be by my side.

As mysteriously as it had appeared, my illness subsided. (It turned out to be a brain tumor I was born with, one that went undetected until it returned to make its latest mischief in 2004.) After all those years of being sick, I turned to skating as a way to reenter life as a normal kid. When I found that I actually enjoyed skating and was good at it, my mom sacrificed everything to make sure that I could continue. She returned to school to get her master's degree so that she could become a professor at Bowling Green University, and became a marital and family counselor, where she was able to do a tremendous amount of good.

It's been nearly three decades since my mother lost her battle with cancer. I know from my mother's experience, and from my own, that nobody wants a cancer diagnosis, and yet, everyone who gets one finds a part of their being that they didn't know existed. It was brutal to watch her in such pain, but as with everything she did, she set an example by showing those around her how to live every last moment and not take anything for granted.

Before she died, she told me, "Some people are given more of life's minutes than others; no matter what, we have to take advantage of the minutes we are given." Mom used her minutes to make life better for her family, her students, and everyone else whose lives she touched. She protected us from seeing any of the anxiety or pain she might have been feeling by finding a way to make us laugh. "Finally, I found a way to lose this weight," she'd say, or "What do you think of my new hair style?" after she went through chemotherapy. She always kept it light and happy, so that we wouldn't worry.

She continued her work helping people through counseling, even when she was very ill. At one point, she was talking with a young couple about to break off their engagement. The woman had lost both breasts to cancer, and even though her fiancé still loved her very much, she felt he deserved better. My mother knew what it felt like to have a mastectomy and to go through cancer treatments, and was able to bolster the young bride's self-esteem. One of the bright spots for my mom at the end of her life was the phone call from that couple, telling her that the wedding was back on.

One of the last things my mother did in her life was to find a sponsor for me, ensuring that I would be able to continue my skating career. She wanted to secure my future, a future that she suspected might not include her. Mom taught me to take responsibility for my talent. She knew I could succeed, and she believed in me, even when I didn't believe in myself. When she died, I threw myself into skating; it seemed like a way that I could honor her with my life, the way she had honored me with hers. I found the answer on the ice. She had sacrificed so much for me to be able to use my talent, and I had been running around acting like I didn't give a damn; the time had come to maximize my gift, so that it didn't go to waste. Winning the Olympic gold medal in Sarajevo was the culmination of all the big dreams my mother had cherished for my career. My performance that night was for her.

Unfortunately, I came up against my own medical challenges later in my life, and although my mother had been gone for many years, she continued to inspire and guide me. When I was diagnosed with cancer, remembering how strong and optimistic and dignified she was when she went through chemotherapy helped me through my own treatment. And when I was diagnosed with a brain tumor, I immediately thought about what my mother would have done. Knowing that she would have found the silver lining gave me a new perspective. Instead of letting cancer (or any of the other terrible losses and heartbreaks that she suffered in her life) bring her down to where she couldn't function, my mother drew strength from these trials, and elevated herself. It was very important to her to keep a very strong face, and to continue to approach life as if every new day was a gift. In doing so, she set a great example for me and others.

Scott Hamilton

Ralf Hotchkiss

*N*avigating a wheelchair along a modern paved street in an American city is very different from riding up a steep hill on a pitted dirt road littered with refuse. Shouldn't the wheelchairs fit the terrain?

That's the question that Ralf Hotchkiss first asked when traveling in Nicaragua in 1980. At 18, he had gone from riding a motorcycle to riding a wheelchair, after an accident left him a paraplegic. In Latin America, he realized that wheelchairs need to be designed to serve the people who use them, taking into account their cultures, their lifestyles, and their landscapes. Over the next two decades, he helped to empower wheelchair riders to design, build, and maintain wheelchairs appropriate for their specific needs, a movement that eventually resulted in the founding of Whirlwind Wheelchair International (WWI). Since 1990, Ralf Hotchkiss and WWI have helped 50,000 riders in 50 countries fulfill the basic need for mobility.

Helen Keller has been my hero since grade school. By the time I finished middle school, I had read, reread, and taken to heart her first book, *The Story of My Life,* written while Helen Keller was still a college student.

Keller was a truly extraordinary woman; in all aspects of her life, she did exactly what she wanted to do. When she lost her sight and hearing before the age of two, she was isolated from the sighted and hearing world. With sheer determination and the help of her teacher Annie Sullivan, she defied the expectations of others, reached out into that world and thrived, turning her world of silence and darkness into one of the brightest spots in history. She traveled all over the world, visiting 35 countries on five continents, and spoke several languages—quite an accomplishment for someone who spent the first decade of her life mute!

I had no disability when I first discovered her works in grade school, but for me Helen Keller was inspiring because she saw every day of her life as an adventure. Her life might have been confined and narrow, but she chose instead to venture as far as possible into the world, setting an example for all of us to follow. As she herself wrote, "Security is mostly a superstition. It does not exist in nature, nor do the children of men as a whole experience it. Avoiding danger is no safer in the long run than outright exposure. . . . To keep our faces toward change and behave like free spirits in the presence of fate is strength undefeatable." That willingness of hers to step into the unknown has carried me through my own life.

Helen Keller's example took on even more significance for me after I broke my back in a motorcycle accident during college. Keller was a leading advocate for those of us with disabilities everywhere; through her personal accomplishments, she taught the world how to see people with disabilities as fellow travelers on equal paths. She came to see her disability as a natural part of her life, and moved on quickly from there. In so doing, she taught me that disabilities aren't insurmountable barriers. They add twists and turns on the road of life, but the road nonetheless stretches out before you if you're game.

Helen Keller not only showed me how it is possible to beat extreme odds, but I learned from her how people with disabilities have used their own experiences and personal adventures to help others. She ignored barriers and fought for the underdog, with a full understanding that the fears and prejudices that imprison people with significant disabilities are much the same as those that cramp social progress and that keep much of the world in dire poverty. And when I had my own chance to help out, I think I took it in part because of her.

In 1980, I was traveling in Nicaragua when I met four young men sharing a single wheelchair. I felt a sudden rush of admiration as I watched their excitement in setting out one at a time—alone—to explore the far corners of Managua. In their explorations the four riders had broken the chair many times, and in repairing it they had made it much stronger. It was perfectly adapted for the bumps and ditches of the country's roads, stronger than any of the ones I had seen in the U.S. The rough terrain had already taken a toll on my high-tech wheelchair and it was beginning to give me some problems. Right away, they pinpointed the problems. I was impressed; they knew more about wheelchair design than wheelchair designers in the U.S., and they weren't letting the terrain or their lack of access to expensive equipment hold them back.

At that moment, I knew I could help more people gain mobility and overcome the roadblocks that the landscape and cultural attitudes put in the way. I had been working on rebuilding my own chairs to fit my needs; now I had found a group capable of designing something that would actually be beneficial to a lot of people. We could work together, design new and better chairs, and pass on the advances in technology to others in developing countries. Now, I get to travel throughout the world, working with wheelchair riders who are inventing and building their own.

Helen Keller is with me on those travels, in my activism, and in my life. It is because of her that I was able to leap into the unknown, and to grab the opportunity to use my own disability to learn from and to help others. As she once wrote, "Life is either a daring adventure, or it is nothing at all."

Ralf Hotchkin

Colonel Jack Jacobs,
U.S. Army (Retired)

*W*hile serving in Vietnam, Colonel Jack C. Jacobs (then 1st Lt. for the 2nd Battalion) was advancing to a combat position on a mission in Kien Phong when they came under intense machine-gun and mortar fire. As the 2nd Battalion deployed into attack formation, devastating fire halted its advance. Due to the intensity of the enemy attack and heavy casualties to the command group, including the company commander, the attack stopped and the friendly troops became disorganized.

Although wounded himself, Lieutenant Jacobs assumed command of the allied company, ordered a withdrawal from the exposed position and established a defensive perimeter. Despite profuse bleeding from head wounds which impaired his vision, Lt. Jacobs, with complete disregard for his safety, returned under intense fire to evacuate a seriously wounded advisor to the safety of a wooded area where he administered lifesaving first aid. He then returned through heavy automatic weapons fire to evacuate the wounded company commander. Jacobs made repeated trips *across the fire-swept open rice paddies evacuating the wounded and their weapons.*

His gallant actions and extraordinary heroism saved the lives of a U.S. advisor and 13 allied soldiers. Through his effort the allied company was restored to an effective fighting unit. For such extraordinary service, he became one of the most highly decorated soldiers to have served in Vietnam, holding three Bronze Stars, two Silver Stars, two Purple Hearts, and the Medal of Honor, the nation's highest combat decoration.

In the words of that citation, ". . . his gallantry and bravery in action in the highest traditions of the military service, has reflected great credit upon himself, his unit, and the U.S. Army."

Heroes tend to pop to the surface during times of crisis. That's why you see so many during wartime, thank God. In a combat situation you find out what people are made of. When I think about heroes, I think of Leo Thorsness, a retired Air Force Colonel who received a Medal of Honor for acts of bravery in dangerous circumstances in North Vietnam—*before* he was captured by the North Vietnamese and spent six years as a prisoner of war, much of the time in solitary confinement, getting beaten every day.

You think to yourself, what would I do in that circumstance? When you talk to men who lived under those conditions, heroes like Colonel Bud Day and John McCain all say the same thing—that they never worried about themselves, but only about whether, under torture, they would betray their country. They'll tell you that a human being can get used to anything, and that anyone would have done what they did under the circumstances.

I'm not sure they're right. I think you have to be a truly tough, single-minded, heroic person to undergo that kind of abuse and still bob to the top. I have complete respect for such men and those attributes, and I am glad I was never in a position to have to find those resources within myself.

Rick Sorenson fought at Kwajalein Atoll in the South Pacific during WWII, and his company came under heavy fire. His heavy machine gunner was killed, his light machine gunner was killed, basically the whole gun section had been knocked out . . . and then he heard someone yell, "Grenade!" He looked down to see the grenade at his feet and made an instantaneous choice: he threw himself on it.

I asked Rick what he was thinking at that moment, when he chose to risk his life to save others. He said, "I knew somebody had to do it, I guess that someone was me." To me, that's the very essence of a hero—an otherwise ordinary person rises to the occasion in a time of great peril, and does what needs to be done.

Combat is a pretty unnatural state of affairs, where crisis is the default mode. Even if the war is going well overall, at the local level it's always a nightmare. In the trenches and on the ground, the chaos doesn't ebb. The truly amazing thing to me is that people *do* rise to the occasion in the midst of all that noise and peril and fear.

In my own combat experience (and I've had plenty of it), whenever there's leadership vacuum, someone always comes to the fore and says, "Follow me." Sometimes it comes from a surprising quarter, and it's the quiet, unassuming guy at the back who suddenly steps up and does what needs to be done.

The tricky thing about being under fire is that doing the right thing doesn't always *feel* like the right thing to do; knowing the difference is what makes a leader. During my first tour in Vietnam, for example, we were walking along a trail in unusually dense jungle, and we got ambushed. Now, your instinct is to drop and return fire, but you're trained to do the exact opposite, to attack immediately *into* the ambush. But even with all our training, in that moment, the instinct to take cover was powerful.

Fortunately for us, a Vietnamese noncommissioned officer stepped up, led us into the teeth of the ambush, and we overwhelmed the enemy. We lost a lot of people in the process, this man included, but if we had followed our instincts, to lie down and try to return fire, every last one of us would have been slaughtered. What he did took tremendous guts—not just to give his own life, as he did, but to lead others on a charge, directly into the face of enemy fire.

If you want to see terrible casualties, follow the guy who is saying, "I don't want to lose anybody." You *have* to drive into the skid; you *have* to drop the nose of your plane when you're losing altitude, even if it feels like you're only speeding the rate at which you are heading into certain disaster; you *have* to attack into the ambush. Don't get me wrong, in combat some loss is inevitable. But if you don't do the right thing, you lose *everything*.

But not all heroism is forged in the crucible of war. Sometimes it isn't so much about putting your life on the line as it is in taking a stand, standing up for what you believe is right.

There's a Medal of Honor recipient whose story stands out in my mind, a man called Lou Millett. He was serving in the Army before the Japanese attacked Pearl Harbor, and he was absolutely incensed that the United States, the great beacon of freedom, refused to fight the Japanese and the Nazis. You have to remember that the war in Asia began in 1931, but the United States steadfastly refused to get involved. In a fireside chat just a few weeks before Pearl Harbor, Roosevelt said that Asian boys would have to fight in Asia and European boys would have to fight in Europe, and that while America would be happy to send planes, trains, automobiles, and other matériel, we weren't sending any of our boys to fight over there. The American position was, "It's not our fight." Of course, it was demonstrated shortly afterward that that was a shortsighted stance to take.

For Lou Millet, even before Pearl Harbor this attitude seemed outrageous. He thought, "This is the United States we're talking about, the cradle of modern freedom. We are supposed to be a principled country, and that means coming to the defense of people who are otherwise helpless. If anyone should be fighting this war, it's us." So he went absent without leave from his American unit and joined a Canadian unit that was fighting in Europe. When the United States joined the war, he went AWOL from his Canadian unit and rejoined his American one. His commander summarily found him guilty of desertion, but instead of sending him to jail, which he could very well have done, he gave him a $52 fine. That was a lot of money in those days for a working soldier, but it was a sum that the commander knew Millet could pay. Millet fought with his unit across Europe and subsequently was awarded the Medal of Honor for acts of heroism in the Korean War.

Now, one can argue with Millet's methods, but you have to respect his decision to take a stand, to say "no, that's not the right thing to do," at a time when it was easy to be comfortable, and comfortable to be easy. Every time somebody says, "Forget about them; that's not our fight" (and they still say it, by the way), I think of Lou Millett.

In wartime, there are plenty of opportunities for ordinary men and women to rise to the occasion, and they do, thank

God. But heroes come from all walks of life. It's ordinary people who make extraordinary events. Anyone who is willing to put it all on the line, and to take a stand for what's right, is as much a hero in my book as a soldier who puts himself at bodily risk to defend his comrades and his country.

Billie Jean King

At a time when women couldn't get a credit card without a man's signature, Billie Jean King was fighting for women's rights in the sports arena and in the women's rights movement. In 1973, a one-on-one challenge from a chauvinistic 55-year-old tennis champion, Bobby Riggs, catalyzed King's campaign for equality. King won the challenge, dubbed the "Battle of the Sexes," with ease.

In addition to her win against Riggs, Billie Jean can add twenty Wimbledon titles, three World Team Tennis championships, the Arthur Ashe Award for Courage (1999), and the Elizabeth Blackwell Award (1998), among others, to her list of awards and accomplishments. The first woman athlete to earn more than $100,000 in one year, King has been honored as Sports Illustrated's *"Sportsperson of the Year" (1973) and as one of* Life *magazine's "100 most influential people of the 20th century." Elton John even wrote a song in her honor* (Philadelphia

Freedom). *She founded the Women's Tennis Association, and played a large part in founding the Women's Sports Foundation and World Team Tennis.*

Billie Jean King's courage to fight for equality on the tennis courts expanded into a crusade to include equal rights for all humanity, regardless of gender, race, mental or physical differences, or sexual preference. Perhaps King's perseverance and strength comes from the adversities that she overcame to become a pioneer in the women's movement and in the tennis world. King's signature glasses corrected her 20/400 vision; she underwent several knee operations; and she endured public press and scrutiny when her bisexuality was revealed.

The L.A. Times *once described Billie Jean King as "a 5'4" 135-pound gladiator for human rights." She's been that and more— a successful tennis player, activist, and businesswoman. These roles have all worked in conjunction with one another for King and for other women. For King, sports participation has a direct relationship to women's success in business. In a 2002 interview on the* Motley Fool *radio show, King said: "Sports are a microcosm of society . . . [and] a reflection of how women are finally having more choices and doing their thing." She continues, "it teaches you character, it teaches you to play by the rules, it teaches you to know what it feels like to win and lose, and it teaches you about life." Whether they recognize it or not, millions of women have been touched by Billie Jean King's philosophy.*

Our lives are shaped by people and events. Most of us are pretty good at documenting, and often celebrating, the important events. And as for the people who shape our lives, they are the heroes (and "sheroes") we carry around in our hearts and souls.

Many people can readily identify one man or one woman who has made a difference in their lives and I applaud those people. Some of us, I believe, are even more fortunate to have a group of people who influenced us. For me, that group includes the teachers who helped me build the person I became. While there were several important teachers in my life, I want to share with you some stories about Mrs. Hunter, Mr. Bamick, and Mrs. Johnson.

The 1950s and 1960s were a great time to experience life. As a kid growing up in Southern California, unlike other parts of the country, it was acceptable, sometimes even encouraged, to take chances and not be afraid to be different from others.

Mrs. Hunter, my third-grade teacher, changed the course of my life. She was an elderly woman but had a youthful soul. While no one would have ever considered Mrs. Hunter a sports activist or enthusiast, she understood how important sports were to me. I still have a report card she sent home to my parents in which she wrote that I had good muscle coordination and was very good under pressure. She encouraged my parents to make sure that I stayed involved in sports, as it was something that motivated me.

Mrs. Hunter had the rare ability to see the best in people and worked hard to make sure she brought that out in each of her students. Since I was a young child, I have had a real love of music and Mrs. Hunter knew that. I remember one day she asked us to take out our pencils and pretend to use them as if we were conducting an orchestra. Let's just say that I was in heaven and I think some of my classmates were as well. Mrs. Hunter had the uncanny ability to home in on a person's strength, and then work to make them feel so good about themselves that they used the strengths they had.

As I grew older I was your typical kid, and while many people may have a hard time believing it, I was actually a little shy. One thing that absolutely terrified me was speaking in public. It was my sixth-grade teacher, Mr. Bamick, who helped me get past that. That year we had to present four oral book reports in front of the class. Some of the kids didn't even flinch, but I was scared to death. Mr. Bamick recognized my fear, so he told me to do a report on a book that was about something that really interested me. So I did the first report on baseball. When it came time for me to present it to the class, Mr. Bamick cut me some slack and let me read the report rather than deliver it from memory. Some of my classmates criticized me for the delivery, but Mr. Bamick defended me. By the end of the year I had completed all four of the oral book reports. It wasn't easy or comfortable for me, but I did it.

Years later I realized that Mr. Bamick did me a tremendous favor in sixth grade. One of the opportunities you get when you win a tennis tournament is to make comments to the fans who attend the match. Some of these are carried live on television and all of them are before thousands of people. It's still not one of my favorite things to do, but, with Mr. Bamick's help, I get through it. A few years ago, I was asked to bring my favorite childhood teacher to a national event in Dallas. I was thrilled when Mr. Bamick joined me for the event. It meant a lot to me that he was there.

I went to high school at Long Beach Poly. This is not your typical high school. *Sports Illustrated* recently noted that more professional athletes have come from Long Beach Poly than any other school in the country. By the time I reached my high school years, I was ranked number two in tennis in the nation and it was time for me to start giving something back to my community.

When I was a sophomore, I offered to do an instructional tennis clinic for students at Long Beach Poly, and, much to my surprise, they turned me down. I was devastated. At this time, girls were only involved in sports sanctioned by the Girls Athletic Association and those were mostly intramural activities.

Not being one to let things lie, I went to Mrs. Johnson, one of the gym teachers at the school, when I was a senior. She let me plead my case, and right away she understood that what I was offering was not about ego, it was about trying to help others. I ended up doing the clinic and sharing some of my experiences away from Long Beach with several of my fellow students. Now, many years later, the Women's Sports Foundation just introduced a program called GoGirlGo that is designed to get inactive girls active. This program will be very successful, and because several of us at the foundation had experiences similar to mine with Mrs. Johnson, we will work hard to make it a success. Mrs. Johnson gave me the courage to push the envelope when the door looked closed, and she showed me the importance of giving back to those around me.

We all need heroes and "sheroes" every day in our lives. They can be role models or they can be important anchors in our world. Mrs. Hunter, Mr. Bamick, and Mrs. Johnson believed in me and they helped me to believe in myself. They taught me the importance of continuing to learn something every day and how rewarding it is to help others. These life experiences and lessons are the things that shape us, the things that make us who we are, and the things that, in the end, are truly important.

Sherry Lansing

Shattering Hollywood's notorious glass ceiling, Sherry Lansing worked her way up from script reader to become the first female head of production at 20th Century Fox. She went on to run Paramount Pictures for fourteen years, where her movies were known as much for the strong women portrayed in them as for their box-office magic. Such iconic movies as Titanic, Fatal Attraction, Kramer vs. Kramer, Chariots of Fire, Forest Gump, *and* Saving Private Ryan *(along with other successes too numerous to name) were all brought into being by the legendary producer Sherry Lansing.*

Lansing resigned from Paramount Pictures in 2005 and is dedicating her "third act" to a life of public service. She has established the Sherry Lansing Foundation, which is committed to raising awareness and funding for cancer research, and also serves on the board of the Carter Center, a not-for-profit human rights organization founded by former president Jimmy Carter and his wife, Rosalynn.

∞

All too often those whom we admire from afar appear less impressive once we get up close. Yet when I met Jimmy Carter, the opposite was true. The closer I got, the more impressive he became.

For as long as I can remember, President Carter has been my hero. I respected him enormously as a president, but for me, where he really distinguished himself was in his post-presidency. Each time I saw him interviewed on television or whenever I read one of his books, I was always struck by the same thought—that he is simply the most decent person that I've ever observed. I saw a man who every day seemed to get up quietly, without any need for self-aggrandizement or publicity, and follow his calling to do good. With the creation of the Carter Center he was able to give that vision global reach. In this President Carter is an inspiration to all of us.

And for me, in a very direct and personal way, he was the inspiration for the next (new) chapter in my life. Some time ago, I determined that when I turned 60, I would stop working at my job and pursue a life of public service. I'm evolving into it and it takes time, but Jimmy Carter is the inspiration for my wanting to do it, and for the way I hope to do it. From his example I know that I can get up in the morning and make a difference just by affecting those around me, by doing whatever I can to make a contribution.

While I was still working at Paramount Pictures, I was fortunate enough to meet my hero. Serendipity struck while I was attending a film festival in Venice. It was at an impromptu lunch, and we were sitting around the table talking about the people we most respect and idolize. I said that the deceased person that I idolized the most was Martin Luther King, Jr., and the living person whom I idolized most was Jimmy Carter. A voice across the table asked, "Would you like to meet President Carter?"

I said, "I sure would." I didn't know the man (who turned out to be Gerald Rafshoon, a member of President Carter's staff), so I didn't know if it was a joke or a serious offer. Sure enough, two weeks later, Jerry calls me at my office and asks if I could come to Atlanta on such and such date to meet Jimmy Carter. "Absolutely," I said without hesitation.

I was overjoyed. I thought I would go and ask him questions like, "Is it stupid to stop your job when, to the outside world, it looks so great?" or "Is it silly to give up a career in the movie industry to pursue a life of public service . . . am I making a mistake?"

I landed in Atlanta at about 11:00 P.M. My meeting with President Carter was at 10:30 the next morning, but I was beginning to get nervous. I called my husband and said, "You know, this is about the dumbest thing I've ever done in my life. This is going to be just like when I met Nelson Mandela." He laughed because when I met Nelson Mandela I was so overwhelmed that I couldn't think of anything to say. The conversation went like this: Me: "I'm so honored to meet you." Pause. Mandela replied, "Nice to meet you, too." Pause. Me: "I'm so honored to meet you." Mandela: "It's very nice to meet you, too, Sherry." I feared that this would happen with Jimmy Carter.

Nonetheless, I arrived at the Carter Center the next morning and was ushered into his office. President Carter was standing, looking out the window. He turned around, and there was this big smile on his face and these twinkly eyes that just were so alive. He said, "I'm so happy to meet you." We sat and talked about everything. The conversation just flowed. His wife, Rosalynn, came in the room and eventually we had lunch. It was extraordinary. Six hours later I left.

Jimmy Carter makes you feel instantly at ease. He's so curious about everything that you're doing, and he makes you feel as if you've known him your whole life. I can't help but think you feel in his presence what people must have felt when they met Gandhi. It is like meeting the kindest, most honorable person in the whole world, who also happens to have a terrific sense of humor. You can absorb wisdom just by being around President Carter, by observing somebody who has no pretension whatsoever and is ruled purely by a desire to help make the world a better place. I learned from him that in my own way I, too, could make a difference. I learned from him that you have to have a passion and care about what you do.

When I left his office that day, I knew that I would leave my job at Paramount at the end of my contract and that I would in some fashion follow in Jimmy Carter's footsteps. My foundation, which educates and sponsors research in cancer and other diseases, is all of four weeks old; all this is sometimes daunting and I have much to learn, but the example of President Carter inspires me and helps to light the way.

These early weeks of starting my foundation have been the best weeks of my life. I look to the Carter Center for inspiration and as a model. Through the Carter Center, Jimmy and Rosalynn have reached out to prevent conflict and improve health throughout the world. The Carter Center focuses on diseases and other domestic and global issues that nobody else is paying attention to or funding. It has attacked river blindness and guinea worm disease, debilitating diseases that have robbed millions of people in Africa and Latin America of the ability to work, attend school, or lead productive lives. President Carter got pharmaceutical companies to donate medicines to treat the diseases and he got other organizations to donate medical supplies. Then he went to these developing countries to assist their governments in distributing those services to citizens.

You don't have to be the president to make a difference.

Yes, it helps to have connections, but to me, President Carter follows his belief system first and foremost and that, more than anything else, is what makes him so effective. He's not dealing with political issues through the Carter Center; he's dealing with global health and human rights. In everything Jimmy Carter does, his charisma, passion, purity, and purpose shine through.

Every Sunday he teaches Sunday school at his church. He has a great marriage. He has great kids. He's a good person, and he's eternally young. He's a painter, a writer, and a fly fisherman. He loves life. His face radiates joy. He has a purpose and a passion; he's not encumbered by all the material things that attract so many people. It's the people who get up and want to give back to others who have the greatest lives. They are not only the ones making a difference, but they have more fun.

Things sometimes come full circle in a funny way. After our initial meeting in Atlanta, President Carter came out to California. We had him over for dinner. His innate curiosity once again in evidence, he was interested in everything and in every single person he met.

About two weeks after I announced that I was leaving Paramount Pictures, I received a phone call from him. I was driving to Long Beach for a preview of *Lemony Snickett,* and President Carter gets on the phone and he says, "Sherry, we just had our board meeting and we unanimously decided that we want you to join the Carter Center board." I burst into tears. To have that kind of validation, and from Jimmy Carter, was monumental. I knew that my decision to leave Paramount and begin my third chapter had been right.

Sherry Lansing

Frances Moore Lappé

They say that "you are what you eat," but few people have made that connection as intimately and in as important a way as Frances Lappé.

While studying food supply at the University of California at Berkeley, Lappé had an epiphany. All of her calculations led her to one conclusion: It is possible to feed and nourish every person in the world if everyone simply eats less meat and more vegetable proteins. Her seminal book, Diet for a Small Planet, *began a movement to create healthier and more efficient ways to nourish people around the globe.*

Lappé's work continues with Food First, which gives the world's poor the resources to feed themselves in an environmentally sound way, and the Small Planet Institute, which encourages ordinary people to creatively engage in civic life by participating in "living democracy." Her work is a reminder that the everyday choices we make—every bite we take—can have tremendous impact. Through those choices, we can help our fellow humans, and actively create the kind of world we want to live in.

Not long ago, I was excited to learn that scientists have discovered "mirror neurons" in our brains. When we watch someone else do something, these neurons fire, just as if we ourselves were doing what the other person is doing. Imagine that! What we observe, we experience. This means that who it is we pay attention to matters. It *really* matters, for we become them.

That's why my attention is on the Kenyan activist Wangari Maathai. In 2004, she joined Nelson Mandela and Jimmy Carter and other world superstars as winners of the Nobel Peace Prize. But she's not my hero because she is now a famous Nobel Laureate, rather, it is because she has modeled what I most want to learn about: power, courage, and hope. Wangari Maathai is my hero because she is The Woman Who Didn't Listen.

In the early 1970s, Wangari—the first woman with a doctorate in biological sciences in East Africa—watched the Sahara desert creep south. In just one century, Kenya's forests had shrunk to less than 5 percent of what they once were. Wangari knew that her country's entire ecology was threatened, with devastating results: villagers, mainly women, had to walk farther and farther to get water and firewood. So

Wangari decided to act. On Earth Day 1977, she planted seven trees, and with that act, launched the Green Belt Movement, a village tree-planting movement whose impact has gone far beyond trees.

When she began, the Kenyan forestry service, established under the British, laughed at her. "What? Untrained village woman planting trees to reverse the encroaching desert? Oh no, that takes trained *foresters*!" But Wangari didn't listen.

"The foresters were not amused," Wangari told us. "They said I was adulterating the profession. I told them, 'We need millions of trees and you foresters are too few, you'll never produce them. So you need to make everyone foresters.' I call the women of the Green Belt Movement foresters without diplomas."

And *because* Wangari didn't listen, Kenya now has 30 million more trees—all planted by untrained village women.

Now that the world has discovered my hero, many laud her unwavering resolve, stunning accomplishments, and her infectious warmth. Wangari, the environmentalist, they call her; Wangari, the human rights and women's rights and pro-democracy activist. All are accurate. But Wangari is my hero because she understands that the true battle is not about rights, as such, or even the environment, as such. She understands that the real battle takes place inside, when ordinary people make that internal shift—as terrifying as it might be—to realize the power that is ours.

"We broke the code," Wangari told me and my daughter Anna when we talked with her in Kenya in 2000. "We told the women: 'Use the methods you know, and if you don't know, invent.' They would use broken pots. They would put the soil and seeds there and watch as they germinate. If they germinate, well and good; if not, try again."

In other words, she told the women to trust themselves.

As the result of her work, tens of thousands of village women who have been taught to defer to chiefs, husbands, colonial authorities, and multinational corporate marketers, and to disparage their own traditions and common sense are now gaining the courage to step into the light. They are saying: *We* have the solutions. *We* can take responsibility. *We* can transform our villages and our nation—and our world.

Wangari told us a story one night in Nairobi that perfectly illuminates this shift in perspective. "I grew up in the Rift Valley," Wangari told us, "and on either side of the valley, there were ridges. I believed that the ridges—where the sky or, quite often, the clouds would reach the mountains—were where the world ended. I believed that what I could see was the whole world.

"Then one day we set out on a journey, the longest of my life. For the first time I came to the top of the ridge, and I discovered there was something beyond. I was so happy to know that the whole world was not in that valley, that there was another world."

"That little journey reminds me of the many, many journeys I have made since. Before you go, you think that the world is just here, and then you go to the ridge and you see there is another world. There are so many ridges in life, and if you are willing to go to the top, you will see another world beyond. But if you don't go—if you don't take the risk—if you only stay where you're safe, then of course you never see past the ridge."

Saying good-bye to Wangari in Kenya five years ago, my heart ached because her movement's funding looked shaky. It ached even more when I got home and learned that she'd been jailed again for her resistance to illegal logging. Friends call me an optimist, but even I would never have imagined, let alone predicted, the changes that just a few years would bring. In 2002, Wangari was swept into Parliament, outpolling her nearest opponent 50 to 1. Soon, she was named Deputy Minister of the Environment, and women danced in the streets of Nairobi for joy.

Green Belt Movement women wear a simple white T-shirt adorned with a simple slogan: "As for me, I've made a choice." Every time I see it, it stirs my heart. This is what Wangari has taught me: To create the world we want, we must choose to act, even when there is no evidence assuring success—even when we face ridicule and loss for our acts.

I used to joke that hope was only for wimps, those folks

without the stomach to face up to how bad things really are. Wangari has taught me the opposite. Hope is reserved for the strong at heart. For hope is not what we find in evidence, I now see. It is what we earn only if we listen to our deepest knowing, and make the choice to act.

Frances Moore Lappé

Leon Lederman

*W*hen not revolutionizing what we know about the physical world, Dr. Leon Max Lederman has devoted much of his prodigious energy and brilliance to improving the state of scientific education in America.

Born in New York City, Dr. Lederman attended public schools and the City College of New York. After receiving his master's degree and doctorate from Columbia University, he stayed on as a professor there, and eventually led the Nevis Laboratories, their center for experimental research in high-energy physics. In 1956, he discovered a new particle; in 1962, with the research that would eventually garner his team a Nobel Prize in Physics, he identified two types of the particles called neutrinos. In 1978, Lederman became director of the Fermi National Accelerator Laboratory, supervising the construction and use of the world's most powerful atom-smasher.

The citations he has received for his scientific brilliance are almost too numerous to list. Dr. Lederman is the recipient of *fellowships from the Ford, Guggenheim, Ernest Kepton Adams, and National Science Foundations. He was a founding member of the High Energy Physics Advisory Panel to the Department of Energy, and the International Committee on Future Accelerators. He has received the National Medal of Science (1965) and the Wolf Prize for Physics (1982), among many other awards and honorary degrees. His astonishing career culminated in his sharing the 1988 Nobel Prize in Physics with Melvin Schwartz and Jack Steinberger.*

Okay, so my hero is my wife Ellen.

My wife as hero? How did that happen? It's not her subscription seats at the Lyric or her total recall of who starred in *Nabucco.* She does have the marvelous ability to forget my jokes, laughing uproariously even though she's heard them over and over again. Is her rare failure of judgment in seeming to admire me what got her nominated? Could the charm of that miscalculation have entrapped me?

Before casting the definitive vote for My Hero, I considered the other candidates. Of course, being a physicist, I thought immediately of my glorious heritage, people like Newton, Faraday, Maxwell, Einstein, Bohr, and others. Yes, each of these could be My Hero, because from each of them (and others, too) we learned about a crucial element in the structure of our physical universe. When you read their biographies, you are struck by how human they were, and the more I read about their battles with colleagues within a system that suffered their individual revolutions poorly, the more I set my own ambitions in their direction.

I also considered those legends I have known firsthand, and who have inspired me personally, like my mentor at Columbia, I. I. Rabi. Teacher, philosopher, and master of the hallway course Charisma 101, he strode the corridors of power with a vision and made it easy for me (and others like me) to do important work. Richard Feynman was the greatest of our contemporary physicists, a beloved and crazy personality, and a true influence. Legends all.

There were also my scientific colleagues to consider—lifelong friends who helped me in our classes and who would inspire me with their depth of understanding during the time that I was relentlessly drowning in a sea of incomprehension. I thank and respect them for their friendship and advice and calming influence, as well as for their capacity for fun. They made the laboratory not just an intellectual foxhole, but the place for a fierce after-dinner Ping-Pong game—a place of pleasure and joy. Why not these heroes?

Or another possibility—a hero not just to the citizens of Chicago, but internationally: the unearthly Michael Jordan. To watch him was ballet, a combination of aerodynamics and sheer magic. Can any of us forget the pleasure he gave us? Were his achievements any less dramatic and important than the tensions and expectation we find in a late Beethoven quartet? He made us want to win, and when it seemed impossible, he went on to show us how.

So how did I come to choose otherwise? Why, with all these candidates, did I choose HER?

She is a horse person, which means she goes from tossing down 60-pound bales of hay to cleaning stalls, from giving injections to pacifying a terrified animal to riding fearlessly for hours along narrow tracks in the Teton Mountains with Sudden Death Canyon on one side. And then, equally fearlessly, she steers the essentials of the dinner party—the table artfully set, six innovative but matched courses, even with no advance notice! (You should taste her sweetbreads or osso bucco.) When our guests arrive, she is organized, dressed to kill, and a natural diplomat as the laureates and novelists and senior government officials take their seats and begin their profound insights into the workings of the physical universe, human consciousness, and necessary cuts in the research budgets. No matter who has shown up in the procession of visitors over the course of our life together, she has charmingly forged casual and informal relationships with them, and has made them feel at home, just as she has always made me feel.

She's a continual learner, and her intellectual curiosity is endlessly renewing itself—and feeding my own. An art photographer, she sets up her tripod and camera and tells me to look through the lens. I don't see what she sees until the black-and-white print appears, and then I become aware of hidden patterns, symmetries and near symmetries, a range of shades from the darkest black—no, there are still discernable shapes in the deepest black—to a brilliant white that can't be due only to the passive photo paper.

Her curiosity and boundless enthusiasm for life open the door for me every day to vistas I might never have otherwise experienced, and make our every day together a renewal. Perhaps it is this capacity to surprise—to show me what I can't see, and to find something hidden and fascinating in every new person and experience—that makes my wife heroic in my eyes. It's certainly how such an intense love can be maintained for so long and be continuously renewed, not just by life's pleasures, but by its crises as well.

Yes, maybe that.

Stan Lee

*S*tan Lee is best known as the creator of the classic super-heroes—as beloved today as they were back in the '50s when these larger-than-life heroes first donned their capes and swooped in to ensure justice and the American way. Today these superheroes are animated, illustrated, mass produced, and blockbusters at the box office. Born Stanley Lieber, he was a voracious reader who as a teenager dreamed of writing the great American novel. So at age sixteen when he joined Marvel Comics he decided to cut his real name in half, to Stan Lee. He was saving the full name for bigger things than "lowly comic books."

One year later, Stan Lee had already made quite a name for himself by becoming the youngest editor in the comic book industry.

He remained at Marvel Comics for over five decades and helped create a pantheon of heroes that has thrilled generation after generation, including *The Incredible Hulk, Iron*

Man, Spider-Man, the Fantastic Four, the X-Men, Daredevil, the Mighty Thor, Doctor Strange, the Silver Surfer, and many more.

One of the trademarks of Stan Lee's superheroes is the fact that they possess not only super powers, but also very human problems and real flaws. While they are not perfect, his characters choose time and again to fight evil in the face of overwhelming obstacles—and win.

My hero is Errol Flynn—not the man himself, whom I never met personally, but the actor who created on-screen personas that captured my imagination as a child in ways that both shaped my character and influenced my future as a writer. So, you might say that my hero is both a real-life person and a fictional character.

Errol Flynn's portrayal of heroes is what appealed to me. He played characters who made a difference and did the right thing, who were bigger than life, and were nobler, braver, and more courageous than anybody I had ever known. I still recall how watching his portrayal of Robin Hood made me wish for the opportunity to rescue women and give to the poor.

Almost every role he played was more admirable than the one before. I'll always remember him as the courageous sheriff of Dodge City and the benevolent pirate, Captain Blood. I had trouble separating the actor from the roles he played when he fought in the Alamo and exhibited valor in the ring as an idealistic, world-champion prizefighter known as Gentleman Jim Corbett.

In virtually every role, any time there was someone in trouble, you could be sure that Errol Flynn would come to the rescue. I'd be so swept up in those movies that, when leaving the theater, I'd stand looking around the street, hoping to find some girl being threatened by a bully—some damsel in distress—whom I could gallantly rescue.

Despite the fact that he played the most virile characters, he imbued those characters with a modesty and a decency that especially impressed me. In every one of his starring vehicles, Errol Flynn was subtly teaching me the virtue of honor. He seemed to personify a man with the most ideal traits: a man of strength and compassion who would never shirk his duty when the need arose.

Anyone who can inspire others to strive to be better human beings is a hero in my book. We normally think of preachers and teachers or even scholars as the sort of role models who lift us up in this way. But sometimes it can be an actor, playing a role, who raises not just our spirit but also our soul.

When I first began writing stories, Errol Flynn and the

sort of heroes he portrayed exerted tremendous influence on my work. Just as he made me long to become a heroic figure who would rush to the aid of people in distress, I likewise wanted to make my audience yearn to be like the heroes in my stories.

Congressman John Lewis

*B*orn *the son of sharecroppers in Alabama, the heart of the seg-regated South, Congressman John Lewis has consistently put his career and his life on the line to fight for a better America, and to protect human rights by the tenets of nonviolence. John Lewis met Dr. Martin Luther King, Jr., when he was eighteen years old, and by age twenty, he had become actively involved in the civil rights movement. As a cofounder and the chairman of the Student Nonviolent Coordinating Committee (SNCC), during the early 1960s Lewis organized sit-in demonstrations at lunch counters in Tennessee.*

As a Freedom Rider, Lewis tested the U.S. Supreme Court ruling banning segregation at interstate bus terminals—and suffered severe beatings by mobs. At twenty-three, Lewis was one of the key planners and a keynote speaker at the historic March on Washington in August 1963. In 1964, he led voter registration drives in Mississippi. In 1965, with the activist Hosea Williams, Lewis led six hundred marchers to the Edmund Pettus Bridge in

Selma, Alabama. Here they were attacked and trampled by Alabama state troopers on horseback and using clubs, whips, and tear gas. Out of this march, which came to be known as Bloody Sunday, was born the historic Selma-to-Montgomery March—and President Lyndon Johnson's decision to sign the Voting Rights Act of 1965 just five months later.

That commitment to civil rights has continued throughout John Lewis's career. He was elected to Congress in November 1986, and is the author, with Michael D'Orso, of Walking with the Wind: A Memoir of the Movement. *In the words of Senator John McCain, "I've seen courage in action on many occasions. I can't say I've seen anyone possess more of it, and use it for any better purpose and to any greater effect, than John Lewis."*

Dr. Martin Luther King, Jr., is my hero. I became a different person, a different human being, as a result of this man and my association with him. When I was a child growing up in rural Alabama, it was my responsibility to care for the chickens on my father's farm. I used to talk to those chickens, preach to them, even baptize them. If you were to look around my office in the U.S. House of Representatives today, you would see that I keep stuffed roosters and brass roosters and ceramic chickens everywhere to remind me of my beginnings. Because if it hadn't been for Martin Luther King, Jr.,

I believe I would still be down there in rural Alabama preaching to those chickens.

I was very young—just fifteen years old, in the 10th grade—when I first heard Dr. King's voice on the radio. His words spoke to my heart, to my very soul. In my religious tradition, people say that someone is "called" to the ministry. That means a voice, a spiritual voice, speaks to that person's soul and says, "You must do something. If you don't do it, no one will. You have to take a stand. You have to speak up. You have to speak out."

That feeling of being called is the only way I can express what I felt that day when I first heard Dr. King on the radio. I felt that he was speaking directly to me—as if he was right in the room, looking me in the eye and using my name. He said that there were people in trouble, that the society was in trouble, and I heard his message of love and nonviolence as a very personal call.

I was open to this message of change. You see, growing up in rural Alabama, I was what Martin Luther King, Jr., used to call "maladjusted to the problems and conditions" of that day. I had tasted the bitter fruits of segregation and racial discrimination, and I didn't like it. It took Martin Luther King, Jr., to make me understand that being maladjusted was a *good thing,* a necessary thing. As a small child, when my family visited the little town of Troy, Alabama, ten miles away from our home, I saw the signs that said, "White

Men," "Colored Men," "White Women," "Colored Women," "White Waiting," "Colored Waiting." I would go downtown to the little theaters from time to time, and all of us little black children had to go upstairs to the balcony, and all of the white children went downstairs to the first floor. I would come home confused and upset and ask my mother, ask my father, my grandparents, my great-grandparents, "Why segregation? Why racial discrimination?" And they would say, "That's the way it is. Don't get in trouble. Don't get in the way."

But when I heard Martin Luther King, Jr.'s voice on the radio that day, I heard a very different message. He was saying, "John Lewis, you need to find a way to get in the way." In the Old Testament, there's a story that says the way a prophet stirs things up is just like the way a mother eagle stirs up her nest to give the little birds the courage to get out and test their wings. Martin Luther King, Jr.'s words on the radio that day agitated me to move, to get out there and stretch my wings. I was being called to get in trouble—good trouble, necessary trouble—and I've been getting in trouble ever since.

I was changed from the moment I first heard Martin Luther King, Jr.'s voice. Before long, I would meet him in person, and that meeting would change the course of my entire life. When it was time for me to go to college, I decided to apply for admission to Troy State College, a small local college near my home. I never received a response. So without anyone knowing it, I wrote a letter to Dr. King, and I told him I wanted to try to desegregate Troy State. Dr. King wrote back to me and sent me a bus ticket to Montgomery.

Finally, on a Saturday morning in March of 1958, my father drove me to the Greyhound bus station, and I boarded a bus and traveled the fifty miles from Troy to Montgomery. When I arrived, a young lawyer named Fred Gray met me there. He had represented Rosa Parks, Dr. King, and the Montgomery movement. He drove me to the First Baptist Church in downtown Montgomery and ushered me into the church office, where I saw Dr. King and the Reverend Ralph Abernathy standing behind a desk.

I was so scared I was shaking, and I didn't know what to say or do. Dr. King spoke up and asked, "Are you the boy from Troy? Are you John Lewis?"

I found the courage to say, "Dr. King, I am John *Robert* Lewis." I gave him my whole name; I wanted him to be sure that he had the right man. That was the beginning of my involvement with Dr. King and the modern-day civil rights movement, an association that would not only change my life but make me a part of something so great that together we changed the destiny of America.

Sometimes, when I look at documentaries of the Movement or I visit one of the civil rights museums, I wonder at the tremendous spirit it took to inspire a people to endure so much and struggle so hard. It took someone like Dr. King to imbue ordinary people with the extraordinary vision to risk everything they had to bring down the walls of segregation. All of us knew that if we got involved in the civil rights movement, we could be beaten, or shot, or killed, but we faced the dogs and the fire hoses because we were longing to be free, and because Dr. King made us believe that it could happen.

Perhaps his greatest lesson to me was that "hate is too heavy a burden to bear." That ethic of nonviolence, that fundamental belief in the transformative power of love, was the philosophy that helped us endure. When someone would beat us, throw us in jail, spit on us, or put lighted cigarettes out in our hair or down our backs, Dr. King's words and his example gave us the strength not to strike back, not to return their hate. I still heed those words today as I interact with my colleagues in the U.S. Congress.

Dr. King preached about the honor in suffering: he told us we had to redeem the soul of America, and in order to do that, we had to be willing to suffer. So, during the height of the Movement, we would remind each other of our convictions and say, "Be prepared to put your body on the line." When a group of thirteen of us, seven whites and six blacks, left Washington, D.C., in May of 1961 to go on the Freedom Rides, we truly didn't know whether we would come back alive. But we were prepared to die, if necessary, for what was right.

I'm the type of human being that I am today, I am the kind of person I am today because of Dr. King. On one occasion he told us, "When a man straightens up his back, no one can ride him." And ever since I first heard those words, I have been trying to straighten up my back—to speak up, to speak out, and to believe in something greater than myself. He freed me by giving me the courage, the know-how, and the tools to strike a blow against racism and bigotry, and the whole society changed because of who he was and what he stood for.

There's a personal story that I think shows something about the distance we've come in America in laying down the burden of race. It's a distance that we could not have traveled—that *I* could not have traveled—without the words, the example, and the influence of Dr. Martin Luther King, Jr.

In 1956, when I was sixteen years old, I took my brothers and sisters and my first cousin down to the Pike County Public Library in the little town of Troy, Alabama, to get a library card. I don't know what possessed me to do it; we could have been lynched just for asking for a library card. But I wanted access to that knowledge, so I decided to test the grip of segregation. The librarian turned us all away that day, explaining that the public library was not for coloreds, but for whites only.

In July of 1998, thirty years later, I went back to that same library. It was in a different building, but it was still the Pike County Public Library. This time I went there, not to sign out a book, but to sign copies of my biography, *Walking with the Wind.* Hundreds of citizens, both black and white, showed up to hear me read and to shake my hand. The librarians there remembered that many, many years before I had been denied the chance to use the services of the public library. That day they not only welcomed me, but they also waited patiently for me to sign their books and gave me a library card.

We have come a long way in America because of Martin Luther King, Jr. He led a disciplined, nonviolent revolution under the rule of law, a revolution of values, a revolution of ideas. We've come a long way, but we still have a distance to go before all of our citizens embrace the idea of a truly interracial democracy, what I like to call the Beloved Community, a nation at peace with itself.

John Lewis

Dr. Bernard Lown

*I*t would not have been a surprise if the renowned cardiologist Dr. Bernard Lown had won the Nobel Prize in Medicine. After all, this Professor Emeritus at Harvard and founder of the prestigious Lown Cardiovascular Center invented the DC defibrillator and the cardiovertor and introduced the use of the drug Lidocaine to regulate disturbances of the heartbeat—research innovations that have unquestionably saved millions of lives.

But the Nobel that Dr. Lown accepted in 1985 was for peace, in acknowledgment of his work on another large-scale lifesaving project: the cofounding, with the Russian physician Dr. Evgeni Chazov, of International Physicians for the Prevention of Nuclear War. The organization now boasts more than 145,000 physicians from 40 countries, brought together to secure what Dr. Lown has called the most fundamental of all rights: the right to survival.

His activism since the Nobel has had an equally profound impact on world health. His international bestseller The Lost Art of Healing *focuses on the unique responsibility of the physician to listen to, engage with, and care for a patient, despite the interference of the economies of medicine. Many physicians believe that it should be required reading at every medical school in the country.*

In response to some of the same issues, Dr. Lown also co-founded the Ad Hoc Committee to Defend Health Care, a not-for-profit organization for physicians who believe that health care is a fundamental human right, and one that should be guided by "science and compassion, not by corporate self-interest."

Dr. Lown's advocacy has global reach. In 1988, he founded SatelLife, an international organization that uses a network of satellites, ground stations, and e-mail to send desperately needed up-to-date medical information to medical professionals in the developing world, where poverty and disease take a terrible toll. Originally conceived as an answer to the Strategic Defense Initiative, which was designed to put weapons of mass destruction into space, this network of lifesaving communication now reaches more than 120 countries and 20,000 individuals.

Whether his focus is on individual hearts, the practice of medicine, or the world itself, this eminent physician embodies the very definition of a healer.

In 1995, I began to think about this matter of heroes and heroism, and what that might mean during this sordid atomic age. If one followed the media, the world was peopled with criminals, rakes, and rogues. Perhaps to make myself feel better, I began to keep a list of people I considered to be heroes, thinking that someday I would write a book about them. The list grew to about sixty-five names, then other tasks displaced this hobby and I forgot about it. When I was asked to participate in this project, I located the list and found it fascinating.

Most of the people on the list are people nobody has ever heard of. People like the artist Gunter Deming, who has placed small brass plaques that he calls "stumbling blocks" outside of the houses of people killed by the Nazis in Cologne, so that as you walk, you can't help but think of the atrocities that transpired, and of German culpability in those atrocities. Or Jules-Gérard Saliège, the Archbishop of Toulouse, who issued the first pastoral letter decrying Vichy policy on the Jews. Or Tamar Golan, the Israeli ambassador to Angola, who stayed on after his appointment to do landmine cleanup with the Angolan government. Or Raphael Lemkin, who spent a lifetime working for the United Nations to adopt the Genocide Convention.

I think of Ahmed Snoussi, a Moroccan comedian who was banned from performing his particular brand of political humor because, as he says, the government cannot laugh and cannot bear to have anyone else laugh either. Imagine—this man's sense of humor has made him an outlaw!

So, when you ask about heroes, clearly I have many—my wife Louise foremost. And I admire many of the people I have had the good fortune to know, like Willie Brandt, Olof Palme, Desmond Tutu, James Grant, Halfdan Mahler, and Mikhail Gorbachev. But if I had to winnow out one person from the many whose moral courage has inspired me over the course of my life, it would be my friend Joseph Rotblat. For me, he is the person who truly embodies what it means to be a hero.

I think of a hero as someone who, over a lifetime, performs deliberate, carefully thought-out, unique acts that demand moral courage. These are acts that anyone *could*, but no one else dares, do. The impact that a single courageous good deed can have is enormous. Just one such action may launch ripples to the eternity of time.

I chose Joseph Rotblat because he took more seriously than anyone I have ever met Einstein's admonition to scientists: "Concerns for man and his fate must always form the chief interest of all technical endeavors. Never forget this in the midst of your diagrams and equations." In 1955, Joseph Rotblat was one of the signatories of the famous Russell-Einstein Anti-Nuclear Manifesto. In 1957, he was cofounder of the Pugwash Conference on Science & World Affairs, one of the leading authoritative bodies on nuclear arms control and disarmament, and in 1958 he cofounded the UK Campaign for Nuclear Disarmament. In 1995, he and the Pugwash movement were the recipients of the Nobel Peace Prize, and he is now Sir Joseph Rotblat—which is all the more interesting because the British government disowned him completely at one time.

Joseph Rotblat was born in 1908 to a wealthy family in Warsaw, but their fortune was destroyed in World War I. By fifteen, he was on his own, completely unschooled and impoverished, and working as an electrician. But he loved books and learning, and studied by himself, eventually applying to the famed Warsaw University. It seemed impossible: there were 55 applicants that year for three spots, and there was a well-established institutional bias against Jews, but despite these obstacles and the fact that the university had never before admitted someone without formal schooling, Rotblat won one of the three openings.

Once accepted, he gravitated to the primitive biologic/radiologic lab as a researcher. He was working with a minute amount of radium in solution with a 27-second half life, but they wouldn't let him move the Geiger counter he needed for his work close to his workstation. So he had to race, carrying his radioactive cargo, three floors down to the basement to use the counter. The only way he could do it in time was if he took entire staircases in a single bound. The University finally permitted him to move the Geiger counter—but only after he'd broken a leg.

Rotblat's brilliance as an investigator meant that his lab

was competing in the discovery of radionuclides with the famous Enrico Fermi's prestigious team, then in Rome. James Chadwick, the Nobel Laureate who had discovered neutrons, took note of the young scientist in Warsaw, and he invited Rotblat to his Liverpool laboratory. Rotblat arrived in England just before September 3, 1939, at the very outbreak of World War II. The Holocaust consumed his entire family, including his wife.

Rotblat was among the first people to comprehend the colossal implications stemming from the fission of uranium. He told me once that his first reflex, when the enormity of it had sunk in, was to put the whole thing out of his mind like the first symptoms of a terrible and fatal disease, in the hope that it would just go away. At the same time, he was absolutely overwhelmed by fear, knowing that the most advanced research in radiation physics and the most seminal discoveries had been made by the Germans. He felt sure that someone in Germany must also have come to the same conclusion, and that they would move ahead with this research to develop some sort of device, with the most devastating consequences.

That conviction led him to accept an invitation from Chadwick to go to Los Alamos as part of the scientific alliance between the British and the Americans proposed during the Roosevelt-Churchill summit in Quebec in 1943. There was a catch—only British citizens were permitted to participate. Although he was immediately offered British citizenship, he turned it down out of respect and loyalty for Poland, which was under savage German occupation at the time. He had hopes that he would eventually return to find his family and to help rebuild that shattered country. General Leslie Groves, the tough-minded director of the Manhattan Project, brooked no deviations. It is a mark of Rotblat's distinction that an exception was made for him.

The act of heroism that defined the rest of his life came in December 1944, while he was working in New Mexico on the Manhattan Project. He concluded that the Germans had abandoned the bomb, which meant that the American justification for this appalling project had vanished; there could simply be no reason to continue building such an infernal device. When he reached that conclusion, he resigned immediately and left Los Alamos. There were two thousand scientists involved, all with the same information—and yet *not one of them* did what he had done.

As a foreigner, he was immediately suspected of disloyalty; he was called a traitor and was investigated for being a Soviet spy. This went on for years, during which time a trunk, filled with memorabilia and photographs of his wife and his family—his only material link to his childhood, his family, and to his homeland—was stolen by intelligence agents and never returned.

Rotblat returned to Britain but couldn't work in physics,

as he could not gain clearance because he was still suspected of being a spy. For many years, he was watched by intelligence services. So he went to work at St. Bartholomew's Hospital, and over the next thirty years became one of the leaders in medical physics, developing international standards for radiation protection. In radiation biology, he remains without peer.

Joseph Rotblat is my hero because, despite surveillance and persecution, he remained utterly unswerving in the quest to rid the world of genocidal weapons. Here's what Bertrand Russell, whom I consider to be one of the finest philosophers of the twentieth century, wrote about Rotblat in his auto-biography: "He can have few rivals in the courage and integrity and complete self-abnegation with which he has given up his own career to devote himself to combating the nuclear peril as well as other, allied evils. If ever these evils are eradicated and international affairs are straightened out, his name should stand very high indeed among the heroes."

Bernard Lown

Wangari Maathai

In 2004, Wangari Maathai received the Nobel Peace Prize for "her contribution to sustainable development, democracy, and peace." She is the first African woman ever to receive the award.

As founder of the Green Belt Movement, an organization that has mobilized thousands of Kenyans, mostly women, to plant more than 30 million trees across the country, Wangari Maathai is responsible for providing much-needed firewood, lumber, shade, and even food to thousands of African families. Now a member of the Kenyan Parliament, she works to spread her message of peace through grassroots mobilization and by stressing that a healthy planet makes peace more plausible.

My life's work has been made possible through the dedication, intelligence, and power of women. It was the women in my life who taught me not only to read and write, but about service and community, the values that guide me still.

Women have an innate sense of service. It is part of who we are. We give rise to new life by nurturing it inside us for nine months. Then we bring it forth and feed it with our own milk, with our own body, and eventually, our own self. My mother was the first strong woman in my life. I know that it was she who instilled in me a true sense of my own power and my responsibility as a woman.

Growing up, I was further influenced by the communities of nuns and missionaries who ran the schools I attended. For me, they exemplified solidarity, dedication, and service. Though I was raised in Kenya, my upbringing was very international. My first set of teachers were Italian nuns, and the second ones Irish (I still want to do a jig when I hear Irish music!). I was impressed that these nuns would leave their own homes and their families to travel to a strange country to educate us, complete strangers. Since childhood, I have wanted to emulate these women because they were not only beautiful, smart, and kind, but also showed me what it meant to dedicate your life to something greater than yourself. For me, that sense of duty and service to the community was a new way of thinking.

In high school I first met Sister Jean Marie, an Irish nun from the order of Loreto who taught science. I still think of her often and was touched to learn that she is buried in Kenya. She and other sisters had given up, in their own words, "the pleasures of the world" to serve God. They believed in the inherent good of all people, and one of the ways they served God and a higher purpose was to give us a good-quality education. Education is a special gift because it continues to grow and multiply. Our people value education, and these missionaries endowed us handsomely in this area.

Sister Jean Marie took me under her wing. After experiments, she would invite me into the laboratory to clean lab equipment and discuss with me the lessons of the day. Her attention actually made me enjoy the sciences. I was already doing well in my studies. But when a teacher pays special attention to a student, the student pays special attention to that class, and I worked extra hard. It was in large part due to her that I decided to focus my studies on the sciences.

I admired certain aspects of nunhood and would probably have become one if I had been raised as a Catholic. Having grown up as a Protestant, there was always another competing voice in my life calling me toward the values of a family. In our culture, you live for your family and especially the next generation. So the whole concept of forsaking family life to live in a convent was completely unknown to us.

So I found another way to serve, out in the world. My mother always told me that from my grandmother, I inherited a strong sense of wanting to put things right. From the nuns I learned a deep sense of seeking justice for myself and for others. I knew that if I could join forces with others and create a community with a goal, then that goal would be met.

So in 1977, we started the Green Belt Movement. Throughout Africa, women are the primary caretakers and users of primary resources. They are responsible for tilling the land and feeding their families. The Green Belt Movement enlists these rural women to address their own needs— a lack of firewood, clean drinking water, balanced diets, shelter, and income—by planting trees. Trees provide fuel, food, shelter, and income to support the children's education and the women's household needs. On the scientific side, they also improve soils and watersheds.

Our work is often difficult and accomplished under hostile conditions. Still, the groups of strong women stayed powerful, and worked toward the common good. Women are my army: I say, if you need to get something done, enlist women to your cause. When times were difficult during the struggle for independence in Kenya, I tried to model myself after the nuns who would come into our rooms in the middle of the night to encourage us not to be afraid when the Mau-Mau attacked nearby. Instead, they encouraged us to engage in prayer. I am quite sure they were afraid, but they didn't show that fear. They told us we were strong because we were together, and we were never harmed.

To this day, I refuse to embrace the fears that stand in my way. I tell myself, "So long as we are working together for good, for service to others, we will not be harmed." And although sometimes we have been jailed, even beaten, we have always stayed together and we have pressed on. Together, the women of the Greenbelt Movement have planted more than 30 million trees—women, nurturing the earth itself.

I am proud to share the credit for my accomplishments with my mother, who gave birth to me, and with all the nuns who shaped my perception of the world and my role in that world. My work is the embodiment of their patience, persistence, and commitment to service.

Wmm Maffai

Wynton Marsalis

*W*hether playing his trumpet, recording sixteen Grammy Award–winning albums, or teaching thousands of students each year, no one in this generation has done more than Wynton Marsalis to enhance, elevate, and export our most American of art forms: the music of jazz.

As a performer and composer, he joins the pantheon of legendary artists such as Louis Armstrong, Duke Ellington, and George Gershwin. His music, played throughout the world, tells the story of American history—invoking our shame, our values, and the painful struggles we've endured. His composition Blood on the Fields *tells the story of slavery and what it means to be free. It won him a Pulitzer Prize.*

He has also worked to ensure that jazz's legacy is permanent. Jazz musicians have been playing at Carnegie Hall as guests since the forties, but always drifted back to smoky clubs and movie soundtracks. Now, thanks to Wynton Marsalis, jazz will *always have a permanent home at one of the world's preeminent performing arts venues, Lincoln Center.*

In addition to composing and performing, Marsalis has made it his mission to turn young musicians on to the joy of jazz, by personally teaching thousands of kids each year. His educational outreach goes even farther through projects such as the award-winning television series Marsalis on Music. *So he is a hero, not just to those who are touched by his music, but to the next generation of artists he so carefully nurtures.*

I never had the chance to meet my hero, Edward Kennedy "Duke" Ellington—legendary composer, arranger, band-leader, and pianist. I have, however, played with a lot of people who played with him. One time I asked the tenor sax player Harold Ashby what it was like. By way of response he showed me the schedule from 1970—Duke was 71 years old at that time—and it was insane; he was traveling on tour every day, and composing every night. As a composer he was remarkably prolific—writing more than 2,000 pieces from symphonic suites to some of the most celebrated classic songs. That work ethic alone is astounding, but what makes him so inspiring is the way he kept developing creatively decade after decade from the '20s to the '70s. No matter how successful he was, he never stopped pushing the envelope, never rested on his laurels. He was just as creative in his seventies as he was when he started his first band at the age of 18.

I didn't listen to Duke Ellington's music until I left home in New Orleans for college in New York. I was about 18 or 19 years old, and that's when I discovered for the first time that jazz could be so sophisticated. Duke's work was an entirely original blend of New Orleans jazz, blues, spirituals, American folk music, and various European forms—a complex brew that was uniquely itself. I was overwhelmed. I started really getting into his music and reading books by and about him, like his autobiography, *Music Is My Mistress*. What came through was his love of life, the depth of his intelligence, his dedication to American music, and his work ethic. He always said the bags under his eyes were the symbols of his virtue: He would stay up all night working on his music. He partied, too; he was justifiably celebrated for that as well.

Any time that something is difficult for me, I think about how Duke Ellington continued productivity under all kinds of relentless pressure: The pressure to keep his band on the road, and to keep it together in the late '40s and '50s when swing era big bands were being overshadowed by bebop and rock and roll. The pressure to keep coming up with ideas, to create music all the time. The pressure of dealing with segregation and ignorance.

Duke Ellington moved to New York at the start of what is

called the Harlem Renaissance. But when he was the featured player at the Cotton Club in Harlem, blacks were only allowed on stage, not in the audience. When he toured, he rented a train with sleepers and dining cars so his musicians wouldn't have to face segregated hotels and restaurants and any other incidental forms of social ignorance. His extended pieces from *Black Brown and Beige* to *A Tone Parallel to Harlem* was the inspiration for my oratorio about slavery, *Blood on the Fields.* That piece details in music what I feel it takes to achieve soul: the willingness to address adversity with elegance. That's what Duke did—address adversity with elegance.

Duke Ellington composed and performed right up until his death in 1974, at the age of 75. He dedicated himself to living a *life of music.* I knew that I wanted that life when I was 12. (I started playing when I was six, but I didn't start practicing until I was 12!) I was always around musicians; my father Ellis Marsalis is a pianist and music educator. He inspired me to become a musician, and he's my hero as a teacher.

When everyone else was saying don't waste your brain on music, musicians don't do anything but struggle, and they can't make any money, my father said, "The only advice I can give you is, if you go into music don't have anything to fall back on. Because if you have something to fall back on, you'll fall back."

From my father and Duke Ellington I learned the value of nonstop learning—I still take the occasional lesson—of practicing, of being a responsible and responsive part of a group, of having a good time, of embracing difficult things. I've won lots of awards, but ceremonial honors, while a lot of fun, aren't that important to me. I think I won more Grammys and things when I was younger. I really never knew why I was winning them back then. With awards you never know. The greatest reward is all those people who bring their kids to me and wait around for me to give them lessons. That's a true award. Sometimes they bring a pie or some cookies and stuff to say thank you.

Senator John McCain

Whether as a prisoner-of-war in a solitary confinement cell in Hanoi, or walking the halls of Congress, Senator John McCain has displayed a sense of honor and justice that has earned the respect of his colleagues on both sides of the aisle.

His service to his country during the Vietnam War stands out as one of the shining examples of heroism during that era. As a member of a prominent navy family, the seriously injured McCain was offered an early release when he was shot down in 1967. Sensing a publicity stunt by the North Vietnamese, McCain cited military protocol and insisted that POWs captured before him be released first. He was held in a prison camp for five and a half years.

McCain won a congressional seat after retiring from the military with a Bronze Star, a Silver Star, a Purple Heart, and a Distinguished Flying Cross for his bravery. A senator since 1986, he has aggressively pursued campaign finance reform, anti-tobacco legislation, lower taxes, a cleaner environment, and more resources for public education—often crafting bipartisan solutions in bitterly partisan surroundings.

In a career of public service that spans almost fifty years, McCain has defined himself by his strong leadership, patriotism, and unswerving allegiance to principle over partisanship.

A friend of mine, Bob Craner, once told me a story of hero worship that was a cautionary tale. He was an ardent and rather obdurate fan of Ted Williams, the great Boston Red Sox slugger and the last man in baseball to hit .400. For a number of years, the hard-hitting St. Louis outfielder, Stan Musial, seven-time National League batting champion, had been considered one of Williams's closest rivals for the claim of best hitter in baseball. Bob, out of blind loyalty to his hero, had nothing but contempt for the popular Musial.

In high school, Bob had had a crush on a girl he wanted to ask out but who he feared might reject him. After several weeks of silently pining away for the object of his affection, he finally screwed up his courage enough to risk rejection. To his great relief she agreed to go to dinner with him, and Bob spent the next few days in excited anticipation of his dream date. When the happy occasion arrived, the two got along quite well, and my friend wondered why he had waited so long to approach her. At some point during their conversation, they declared their mutual love of baseball, which only enhanced the young lady's charms in the eyes of my love-struck friend, until, that is, she dropped her bombshell.

"I think Stan Musial is the greatest hitter in the game," she said.

Bob ended the story there.

"What did you say to her," I asked.

"Nothing," he responded.

"Nothing?"

"Nothing. I never spoke to her again."

You have to be careful about heroes. They can affect your life profoundly, sometimes in ways they wouldn't wish to. And you have to be especially careful not to let your admiration for their virtues blind you to their flaws or, as has often happened with me, transform those flaws into virtues.

Ted Williams was my hero, too. There was much to admire about him, but as Ted himself would acknowledge, there were some aspects of his personality that weren't usually considered virtues.

I was a boy when I first saw him at the plate. Allowing that my memory might have embellished the experience to suit my admiration for Ted, I recall that he hit two doubles and a home run that day. But it was a strikeout that I remember most vividly.

It was an away game. The Red Sox were playing the Senators at Griffith Stadium in Washington. When Ted swung at and missed a third strike, the Washington fans filled the ballpark with boos and catcalls. Ted turned toward the crowd and the boxes where the sportswriters who often gave him a hard time were enjoying the spectacle. Then he raised his head, stared defiantly at his tormentors, and spit in their general direction.

I loved him. He was in my estimation the greatest hitter in baseball, the greatest of all time for that matter. But the accomplishments of his legendary career were far from the only thing that attracted my admiration. He was a Marine aviator and decorated veteran of two wars. He was an exceptionally good pilot. He was playing his fourth season in the major leagues when he was called up for World War II. The year before he had hit .406. On opening day in 1942, he hit a home run his first at-bat. At the end of the season he reported for duty, after he had won his first triple crown for the best batting average, most runs batted in, and the most home runs. No telling what he might have done during the three seasons he missed while on active duty. He didn't get a hit his first at-bat after returning from the war. He hit a home run on his second trip to the plate.

In Korea, he had flown in the same squadron as John Glenn, who called him the best natural pilot he had ever seen. He hadn't wanted to go when they called him back to active duty in 1952. He was thirty-three years old, and had a wife and daughter to support. He had also shattered his left elbow during the All-Star game that year when he ran into the fence chasing a fly ball. But he went to Korea and did his duty. Most people assumed he would never play professional baseball again. On one combat mission, enemy antiaircraft fire hit his plane, and disabled its hydraulics. With his plane on fire he couldn't get his landing gear down. Ground control radioed him to eject. He should have, but instead he managed a wheels-up landing with his plane engulfed in flames, an act that took extraordinary skill and courage.

He was six feet four. He knew if he ejected his long legs would hit the instrument panel, breaking his knees. "I would rather have died," he said, "than never to have played baseball again."

I admired his courage and patriotism. I admired his astonishing accomplishments as a ball player. There is something in my character that is attracted to people with a strong independent streak in their personality. I liked rebels, particularly when I was young. And that is what I really liked about Ted Williams.

Later in life, I learned to keep that quality in perspective. Being defiant sorts, persons who go their own way are fine as long as they serve some greater purpose than their own vanity. Oftentimes, my own rebelliousness was simply self-indulgence. And I can't say I'm proud of that today.

I don't know what made Ted Williams so defiant, so adamantly his own man. He had had a tough childhood. He had a temper. And, by his own admission, he had "always been a problem guy." I'm not sure his individualism was always connected to some higher purpose than his own satisfaction. I don't think Ted thought it was. But when I was young, I thought him to be the toughest, feistiest, most independent man I had ever seen, and I loved him for it.

He had a bad year in 1954, suffered several injuries, and decided to retire at the end of the season. He was thirty-six years old, and well past his prime. He changed his mind and rejoined the Red Sox the following spring, but injuries plagued him for the next two seasons. Then in 1957, clearly aging, still battling with fans and sportswriters, still making trouble for himself, he hit .388 for the season, the best record since he had broken .400 in 1941. He won the league batting title that year. He won it the next year, too, when he was forty and hit .328. In 1959, he threw his bat in anger at striking out. It hit a lady in the stands, and Ted was ashamed of himself. The crowd's boos were deafening. Then he hit a double his next at-bat.

For all his well-publicized temper and feuds, he was a kindhearted man. He worked tirelessly and without publicity to raise money for a children's cancer research clinic. Whenever a child with cancer wanted to see him, he came, alone.

In 1960, well into his forties, he decided to give up baseball. Age and injuries had slowed him, and the pressure he felt all his career to be the best was too much to handle anymore. He was as controversial as ever. When he stepped to the plate for the last at-bat of his career, the fans who often got mad at him, but who loved him, and who—he would later admit—he loved, stood on their feet to pay respect to the Splendid Splinter. He hit a home run. The crowd roared for him to come out of the dugout after he had run the bases. They wanted to acknowledge him, and they wanted him to acknowledge their love for him. They wanted him to tip his hat. He wouldn't do it.

He left Fenway Park that afternoon, glad he had played ball and glad to be done with it. He loved the game, but he had played it the hard way, the lonely way, his own way. He had served his country with courage. He had given the game his best. The man who wouldn't tip his hat had been the greatest hitter who ever lived.

John McCain

Ralph Nader

Without Ralph Nader's reforms our America would look very different. Because of Nader, we're confident as we bite into our burgers because we know the meat is safe. Nader's efforts made sure you wouldn't be putting your baby down to sleep in flammable pajamas, or spooning MSG-spiked food into her hungry mouth. Thanks to him, your new car comes with safety features so standard we don't even think about them, like seatbelts, padded dashboards, and air bags. Without Nader, there'd be no Environmental Protection Agency to safeguard the environment, no Occupational Safety and Health Agency to protect workers, no Freedom of Information Act to ensure an accountable government.

For forty years, Ralph Nader has lobbied relentlessly and effectively on behalf of the ordinary American consumer. His reforms on behalf of consumers have reached across issues as disparate as insurance rates, campaign finance reform, the two-party political system, and the lead apron you wear when your dentist takes X-rays. He has said that "real patriotism is caring enough about your country to roll up your sleeves and do something to make it more humane, moral, and caring." It is as precise a definition as you can find of Ralph Nader's own life's work.

My big brother, Shafeek (Arabic for "the compassionate one"), was my hero from birth when he gave me my first name, to the delight of our parents. He was eight years older than I—almost to the day—and the oldest of the four children (two girls and two boys) in our family.

Shaf was an idea factory with many subdivisions. Always the listener, reader, and conversationalist, he was blessed with an absorptive curiosity, and he readily shared everything he learned or thought with the family. I remember once before he returned to his studies at the University of Toronto, he left me a note and three books to read. One was *A Short History of the World,* another was a small philosophy volume by James Harvey Robinson, and the third was a book about music. It was pretty heady material for an eighth grader—so much so that I read every page of each book.

He was a constant local explorer in rural Connecticut and Massachusetts. Countless times he would have us hop into his jalopy and bounce along the side roads (sometimes dirt roads) of the countryside, while he pointed out historic sites, glorious hidden meadows and marshes, and lead us on climbs in the Litchfield country hills, from which we enjoyed spectacular views. Then there was the magic of being woken up in the middle of the summer night for a ride, pajamas and all, to the nearby Hartford reservoir to view the full moon in all its splendor. Later, he argued for education that hones the civic skills of students in the elementary and high schools. He wanted children to learn their own area's history and geography and to explore their own hometowns.

Wiser than his age and more mature than his contemporaries growing up, Shaf paid close attention to his younger siblings—Claire, Laura, and me. With unusual empathy, Shaf was an arm-around-the-shoulder kind of older brother, comforting us in our moments of worry, pain, and anxiety, and celebrating with us our joys. He also brought us down to earth when we became too elated or agitated. But it was the way he counseled or cautioned us that was so effective. He would use analogies from historic figures, or cite his own previous mistakes so that we could learn from them. In so doing, he gave us larger frames of reference, which a narrowly focused preteen or early teenager often needs.

It was not just my parents, sisters, and I who learned so much from Shaf. From his days in the navy during World War II to his many ideas, proposals, and projects afterward, his suggestions were adopted by many people and he was glad to let them take the credit. He would often go to the local town meetings and lay before the elected officials basic solutions to the town's problems, while offering a vision of new horizons for what our town could become. In this vein, he talked up, to much initial skepticism, the formation of a community college. At the time, no town with a population of just over 10,000 people like Winstead had one. Shaf organized a core group of his friends to establish the Northwestern Connecticut Community College; this thriving institution celebrated in its 40th year in 2005.

My brother was interested in structures and systems that were innovative and open to the citizenry, regardless of their power and income. (For instance, he did not like professional spectator sports, but instead urged people to participate in their favorite game.) This interest is one reason why he admired consumer cooperatives, including arts and crafts. Co-ops help build a community and its self-reliance. He thought that our town should have its own ocean fishing boat and its own nearby fresh vegetable farm, under cooperative entities.

Shaf was all about the roots and fundamentals, whether it was the roots of words, or the crucial focus on community in many of its meanings—material, spiritual, nurturing, pioneering, and environmental. He rarely separated people from their locale. Never have I met anyone besides Shaf who could converse so authentically with so many kinds of people from all backgrounds. From them he learned about their felt needs; their viewpoints; their sense of fun, pun, and play; and their yearnings.

His passing at age sixty left us with memories that now serve as guides and lessons, and we established an educational foundation—the Shafeek Nader Trust for the Community Interest—to carry on his civic values and humane work. His wisdom gave us a fundamental sense of priorities for how we can make a difference and work toward building a better community and a better world. I think often of the story of a small moment that took place while he was fighting his final battle against cancer in a California hospital. One day, an African-American nurse who was pushing his wheelchair down the corridor leaned down and said, "I hear your family is for the people."

Shaf replied, "Maybe that is because we are of the people."

Ralph Nader

Paul Newman

Prior to 1982, Paul Newman was celebrated for his blue eyes, handsome good looks, and a body of work rivaling that of any leading man, including such classics as Butch Cassidy and the Sundance Kid, The Hustler, *and* The Color of Money, *for which he won an Academy Award.*

But then the public discovered another talent: Newman had a way with salad dressing. His oil-and-vinegar that he once presented as gifts for friends would become the first in Newman's Own sensationally profitable product line. Newman's Own donates all profits after taxes to educational and charitable funds—adding up to a grand total of more than $150 million since the company's start. As Newman himself has said, "From salad dressing, all blessings flow."

In 1986; Paul Newman founded the Hole in the Wall Gang Camp with Ursula Gwynne and A. E. Hotchner. These free-of-charge camps offer fun and magical experiences to young people living with cancer and other life-threatening blood illnesses, giv-

*ing them the opportunity to leave the sterile hospital environ-
ment behind and to be in the company of other kids facing the
same issues.*

*Newman's longstanding marriage to the Oscar-winning ac-
tress Joanne Woodward, an exception to the Hollywood rule, has
only made him seem more of a role model and quiet leader. He
credits luck for his long and stunning list of successes in life, but
it is the choices he's made with the hand he was dealt that distin-
guishes him as one the best of humanity.*

On a messy winter day in 1931, in the middle of the Great
Depression, my father, Arthur Newman—looking as gray as
the day itself—left house and family and headed for Chicago
to try to negotiate with Spalding and Wilson, the two giant
sporting goods manufacturers, to get sports equipment on
consignment. My father and his brother owned The New-
man-Stern Company of Cleveland, Ohio, purveyor of sports
equipment since 1915, a surviving company in the "luxury"
arena of retailing which would see an 80 percent failure rate
before the Depression ended. Goods on consignment would
be difficult to bargain for in good times, so it seemed almost
impossible to expect success in bad, because the manufacturers would only be paid as the goods were sold and not upon
delivery. A dicey deal to monitor. Money was scarce.

My father came home two days later with a letter of agreement from both manufacturers for $100,000 worth of goods on consignment, a staggering amount in those days, especially under the economic circumstances. But those manufacturers knew that if The Newman-Stern Company sold a baseball glove for nine dollars and ninety-five cents, the manufacturer would have a check in the mail from my father the next day for the five dollars owed them. Such was the reputation of The Newman-Stern Company and the gentlemen who ran it. The business survived and so did we.

I learned a great deal by my father's example and have tried to measure up. I learned from him that honesty is the best medicine. It nourishes the soul, and at the same time, it keeps meat and potatoes on the table.

Stan O'Neal

As chairman, president, and CEO of one of the world's leading financial management and advisory firms, Stan O'Neal is one of Wall Street's most influential executives, and the first African-American to hold a top position on the Street. He is known not simply for turning around the trillion-dollar Merrill Lynch, but also for his extraordinary leadership and integrity—qualities in great demand and short supply these days.

O'Neal's route to the top has been a steady but steep climb, from picking corn and cotton in the fields of Alabama, to working as foreman on the graveyard shift at a General Motors plant, to the top position at Merrill Lynch. He credits his success to his education, which has led him to advocate aggressively for better education for all young people.

Some people are born with a spark. My grandfather, James Isom, not only had that spark, but also the ability to fan it into flames. If he had been born in a different time, I feel confident that my grandfather would have been widely known for his accomplishments. As it is, his memory is cherished by my family and the people in the community where he lived.

My grandfather was born a slave. When he was three years old, President Lincoln passed the Emancipation Proclamation, and in a short time my grandfather and his family were set free. But they had no education, no land, and no tools with which to make a living. My grandfather figured out a way to overcome these formidable obstacles. It was rare in those days for a black man to start his own business, but he did, and became the only black man in the area to own a cotton gin. Whites in the area refused to sell land to him because he was black, but he ultimately became a significant landowner in Wedowee, Alabama, amassing more than 360 acres. He worked his land himself. Each day, he would clear an acre with a mule and a plow, and each night he would plant the freshly plowed field. The next day, he would start all over again.

It's an amazing honor to have a man of this caliber and character as part of my heritage. I like to think that my grandfather left his genetic imprint on me, but it's his legacy in the form of the many stories that were told about him that I try to pass on to my own children. No one knows if these stories are accurate or not, but they're consistent with the person my family knew him to be. For instance, there is a story about my grandfather and the Ku Klux Klan. Someone told him that they would be coming to his home, so he stood vigil all night, alone with a gun, and when they showed up he ran them off. That's the kind of man he was.

My grandfather was self-educated, but he had the vision and foresight to donate part of his land for the founding of The Woodville School, which I would later attend. It was a one-room structure with a wood-burning stove, and it offered an education for kindergarten through sixth grade. There weren't a lot of students, and it lacked facilities and support systems that other, larger schools had, but it offered the first formal education that anyone in the community had experienced. Before it, the black kids in this rural, segregated area had no school at all.

I've gotten to go a lot of places in my life. The other people in my family didn't have the same opportunities that I had, and I know that if I had been born thirty years earlier, I wouldn't have had them either. Many of the people I grew up with never left the small rural community in which I spent my childhood. My father moved our family to Atlanta when I was about thirteen, and it was incredibly fortunate that we were able to leave. As important as my grandfather's school was to the community, it would not have given me the opportunities that the schools in Atlanta gave me.

Some of what I have achieved is the result of luck and circumstance. But some of it comes from the hard work and determination that I saw were part of my grandfather's daily life. He had to be smart, and he had to work very hard. From him, I learned that it is possible to beat the odds. He knew that he faced certain disadvantages, but he accepted them, not as a limitation, but as something to overcome. He taught me that you have to be willing to take responsibility for your situation and not make excuses for yourself. With those principles in place, he made truly amazing things happen by sheer force of will.

Grandfather used to tell me that I could grow up to be somebody great. Whether he truly believed it or was just saying it to instill a sense of confidence in me, I'll never know, but I took him at his word, and his encouragement made an indelible impression on me. In large part, I attribute who I have become to him. I credit him with instilling in me a strong work ethic, a sense of integrity, and a sense of responsibility to always do my best.

Raffi

If you've had a child—or been one—in the last thirty years, you know Raffi Cavoukian, or Raffi, as he is known to millions. His award-winning songs like "Baby Beluga" and "It Takes a Village" teach children and adults about the role they play in the ecological web that connects us all to one another. Sophisticated music and lyrics make his music a delight for child and adult alike.

Raffi has earned many honors for his work, including the Order of Canada and the United Nations' Earth Achievement Award. Raffi's mission is to inspire and educate parents, teachers, and businesspeople to honor the children in their lives and the children of the world. His songwriting is intended to inspire a global attitude that is "child honoring," for only then can we hope to achieve a truly enlightened society. Raffi is committed to raising awareness about the fundamental rights of all children everywhere to enjoy such basic necessities as safe neighborhoods, clean air and water, and the care of loving grown-ups.

We heard it from Mandela, turn this world around
For the children—turn this world around
He's done it once before, and now we hear his call
For the children—turn this world around

The dreams of our young ones born into this world
Need respect and love to come alive
Honoring the children is what we're here to do
Now is the hour and we've got the power to

Turn, turn, turn, turn this world around
For the children—turn this world around
      —from Raffi's song "Turn This World Around"
      (A Song for Nelson Mandela)

At the launch of the Say Yes to Children campaign in 2000, my hero Nelson Mandela said it was not enough for world leaders to continue to spout rhetoric. What we need, he said, is to "turn this world around—for the children!" This inspired me to write a song I hoped would become a rallying cry to help create a child-honoring world—a world that truly honors its young.

What inspires me most about Mandela is the way this tenacious freedom fighter spent twenty-six years in captivity without becoming bitter or demeaning his jailers; refused two offers to be set free on the principle that only free persons can enter into a contract; triumphed over the temptation for revenge; mastered his own lion-heart; and with it confounded his captors such that *they* felt captive—to their stark injustice. Like the Berlin Wall and the Iron Curtain, apartheid, that once impregnable and violent partitioning of people by the color of their skin, disintegrated over time and crumbled, outdone by an unbeatable color-blind foe.

Despite tremendous outward oppression Mandela remained unbeaten and unbowed. That achievement is so striking because he had to resist not only the assaults of his captors but the temptation to surrender to anger, bitterness, and hatred.

His is also a story of the indomitable spirit of South Africans who prevailed at long last over insurmountable odds, by sheer determination, by faith in the vision of a unified homeland, by the grace of music and celebration they kept alive in the darkest of their times. South Africa's triumph is testimony to the power of mind and heart over despair. A boxer turned champion peacemaker inspired a nation of believers and won the support of a world of sympathizers.

Human history is rarely as compelling as when we can see how the actions of one person can move so many and change so much. Nelson Mandela was awarded the Nobel Peace

Prize in 1992 and has received more than 50 honorary degrees from universities all over the world. Yet, even in triumph, Mandela has maintained a humble demeanor that marks this uncommon man with the common touch, father of a nation, hero in a turbulent age.

Mandela is that rarity among public figures, the one who stays true to his origins, true to his calling—in his case, to a lifelong pursuit of social justice. Even in elderhood Mandela has not retired from public life. He works tirelessly to address the state of the world's children, to "turn this world around."

Raffi

Ron Reagan

Ron Reagan may be best known as the younger son of our forti-eth president, but he may be best admired for his courage to speak out for what he believes. Ron Reagan is an avid spokesperson for stem cell research, going so far as to speak at the 2004 Demo-cratic National Convention to promote his cause. It is important to him to see advances in medical therapy for diabetes, Parkin-son's, and the Alzheimer's that claimed his father, President Ronald Reagan, as well as for other diseases. When Ron Reagan argues against President George W. Bush or breaks from his family's roots in the Republican Party, the potential for cures far exceeds the potential rifts.

A registered Independent from one of the most beloved Repub-lican families, Ron Reagan says, "I have no choice but to speak for myself. It's all I've got; nobody's telling me what to say." As his father taught by exemplifying kindness and respect, Ron teaches us a lesson in the importance of speaking up.

What I learned from my father is that it doesn't matter who you are, but how you act. What counts is your kindness and gentleness, and your ability to forgive. Those are the qualities that really define each of us, and separate out the true heroes.

By virtue of his position in life, my father was a powerful person as far back as I can remember, and in two exceptionally heady worlds—Hollywood and politics. Yet my father never let any of it go to his head and he never let it corrupt his core sensibility, which was all about decency.

From Hollywood to the White House, growing up my father's son meant always living in the midst of famous people, and I saw early and often just how arrogant the famous can be. So I learned at a tender age that people may possess truly impressive talents for which they are highly celebrated, yet still fall short as human beings. If you don't treat people with decency, then how important is it really that you can perform extraordinary feats on a football field, or that you've won an armful of Oscars?

In my entire life, I never saw my father, for all the power he had, either as an actor or as president, yell at anyone. No matter what you did or who you were—the Prime Minister, the Queen, or the guy who shined his shoes or cut his hair—my father extended to everyone the same courtesy and respect, treating everyone the same.

In addition to these fundamental lessons in character, I also learned from my father about empathy and compassion—the two qualities that I value above all others. Whenever as kids growing up we would be irate at somebody for some real or imagined transgression, he'd always ask us to flip the coin, and consider the other person's vantage point. "For all you know this person was having the worst day of their whole life. Perhaps something tragic happened, and they suffered some terrible loss. So, perhaps you need to cut them a little slack."

The capacity for true compassion, and the ability to share another person's pain, that's the stuff that really counts (not the window dressing of status and celebrity). Look at any of the great religions and philosophies throughout history and you'll always find—across the board—the same big three: empathy, compassion, and forgiveness. It really does all come down to "doing unto others as you would have done unto you."

So, I guess I'd have to say that it was my father who instilled in me an appreciation for the qualities that I consider to be the true measure of heroes. But it is the Tibetan monks living in China, more than anyone else, who are true heroes to me. The monks' empathy, compassion, and amazing ability to forgive truly inspire me. They have seen the genocide of their people, their monasteries destroyed, and a sacred way of life desiccated at the hands of the Chinese. Over the years they have been tortured and brutalized, but instead of being angry, resentful and vengeful, they forgive their tormentors. The monks feel compassion for those seeking to achieve their demise. They see their tormentors as beings of suffering and delusion who are heaping problems onto themselves.

I saw my father's own capacity to achieve such transcendent forgiveness. After being shot by John Hinckley, my father almost immediately forgave him. Pope John Paul II forgave his would-be assassin as well. Nelson Mandela forgave, most eloquently and in public, the injustice he suffered at the hands of his captors, as terrible as those injustices were. He did so not only for his own redemption but also for that of his country. To call forth compassion when you are facing great torment is to me the sign of true strength and character.

As for me, I see myself as a work in progress. I still have to remind myself to be more understanding. I still lose my temper, and I struggle to forgive people. It doesn't come naturally. And I often chide myself after the fact when I have lost my temper. Looking to my father, the Tibetan monks, and Nelson Mandela, I see the qualities that I most admire in heroes and I have come to count on them, my heroes, to light the way and to show me the right thing to do.

Dana Reeve

A popular actress of stage and television, Dana Reeve was beloved in myriad roles, yet no scripted role could ever elicit such stunning range—of endurance, courage, grace, and grit—as she has come to assume in real life. We all watched the fairy tale unfold: Golden Girl meets Golden Boy; they marry and get that rare chance to live out the sort of picture-perfect existence normally reserved for the silver screen. He was the quintessential romantic leading man, she a gorgeous and talented actress in her own right; they were the couple who literally had it all.

Most married couples vow to remain true to their spouses both in sickness and in health, yet it is hard to imagine the sickness part—especially if your spouse plays Superman. Yet this fairy tale took a tragic turn when a fall from a horse left Christopher Reeve paralyzed from the neck down. We watched in awe as he rose again to great heights: acting, directing, championing the rights of those with disabilities, and tirelessly pushing the frontiers of medicine to find a cure. Where did he find such strength?

Christopher Reeve often credited his wife, Dana, with having given him the strength to rise to the unimaginable challenges he faced after his accident. Through it all, Dana Reeve remained a steadfast and loving wife and mother, while also assuming a pivotal new role as a motivational speaker and activist on behalf of the disabled and stem cell research.

Reeve is a cofounder of the Christopher Reeve Paralysis Foundation, which funds scientists working in spinal cord research, awards money through its Quality of Life Grants program to organizations that improve the daily life of the disabled, and provides information and support to the paralyzed community through the Christopher and Dana Reeve Paralysis Resource Center. Reeve has acted as Chair since her husband's death in 2004. She is the author of the bestselling book Care Packages: Letters to Christopher Reeve from Strangers and Other Friends, *and narrates the audio version of* Dewey Doo-it Helps Owlie Fly Again, *the children's book inspired by her husband.*

(The following is based on a telephone interview with Dana Reeve.)

The hero of my life was, is, and forever shall be my husband, Christopher. Chris is a hero to me for all the reasons that he was a hero to other people. Like everyone else, I admired his courage, his perseverance, the way he handled adversity with grace, and his commitment to better the world in which we live. I was privileged to know him in a more private context as well, where his heroism extended to the way he treated his family and the people closest to him. And I observed at what tremendous cost his courage and perseverance came.

Before his injury, I would have said that Chris was not my hero as much as he was my husband, my friend, my confidant, my lover, my partner, and the father of our child. In many ways he changed after the accident; we both did. Luckily, he was always remarkably open to change, and able to evolve and to adapt in ways that not everybody can. But the personal qualities that enabled him to rise to the challenges he was presented with—not just living with his own disability, but becoming an advocate for all disabled people and a powerful force for change—those qualities were always there. In fact, they were many of the reasons why I fell in love with him in the first place.

The public's response to Chris's injury allowed me to step back a bit, so I could see a little more objectively what a truly great man he was. People were often surprised by how much energy he had for all his advocacy efforts, such as the Christopher Reeve Foundation—an enterprise we founded together—in addition to his work as an actor and director. Chris was an incredible achiever. He was always someone who set the highest standards for himself. When he pursued something, he pursued it fully, and when he decided he was going to do something, he did it at the highest possible level. This was true in every area of his life, including recreation; when you went sailing with Chris, you didn't just float around. For him, enjoyment and satisfaction came from setting goals and achieving them, from doing things well.

Chris was always a natural leader. After his accident, people started turning to him for answers and support—even people who had been injured and had been living with a disability for a long time. Although life with a disability was new territory for Chris, and for me, he was suddenly thrust into the role that he would thrive in—acting as a source of true inspiration and information.

Chris's strength, courage, forthrightness, and natural leadership skills—the same qualities, in fact, that made him so utterly convincing as Superman—served as guides for us and many others as we navigated the challenging roads of living with a disability.

After the injury, some of the challenges Chris faced on a daily basis were pretty significant, bigger than many people face in a lifetime. But Chris took a very proactive approach to these challenges and viewed them simply as problems to be solved. I think this problem-solving mind-set was really what kick-started his activism. He had always lent his support to causes he believed in, including a lot of environmental work as well as appearances for the Special Olympics, Save the

Children, and organizations to fund pediatric AIDS research. The work he did in the nine and a half years following his accident has had an enormous impact on the lives of the disabled in this country and around the world.

That work in good measure all grew out of the question that gnawed at him: "I've got a big problem here. How do I get out of this?" Very quickly, "How do I get out of this," turned into action: "Who do we talk to? Who do we lobby? Whose research can we fund? How can I make a difference in other people's lives?"

I derived a tremendous amount of strength from him, and as a couple, we depended equally on each other. Everyone will face some kind of loss or adversity in life, at some time or other, and often it can completely derail a relationship. People tend to be both surprised and encouraged by the fact that our marriage was so strong. We had a powerful sense of commitment to one another that was fueled by deep love, mutual respect, optimism, and the ability to change with each other's changes.

Maybe the most influential factor was that Chris never stopped participating as a full partner in our marriage. It was a conscious effort made by both of us; we started talking about it when he was still in rehab. As loving as our relationship was, we had always been very healthily demanding of one another in terms of making sure that each person was meeting the other's needs in the relationship. As much as possible, we didn't let that change after the accident. Although I was a caregiver to Chris, I was his wife first, and Chris worked hard to be the best possible husband to me. I believe that's heroic in and of itself and just one example of the heroism he brought to ordinary, daily life.

Chris was heroic as a father as well. No matter how he felt, physically or emotionally, he protected his children, allowing them to live their lives without the burden of worrying about him. Despite the difficulties that challenged Chris daily, he remained a powerful and positive role model in his children's lives.

Chris continues to inspire me every day, even now that he's gone. When he died, the board of directors asked me to step in to take over the chairmanship of the Christopher Reeve Foundation. That had always been Chris's job, a job I had never aspired to, and to be honest, I was initially ambivalent about taking it. But a friend of mine said to me, "You know, Chris didn't want to be paralyzed, but look what he did with what was handed to him. Use him as your motivating force." My friend was right. The work Chris started is too important to stop now; and I have taken on the mission to make sure that the momentum he built doesn't peter out. The Christopher Reeve Foundation will continue funding the best scientists, and the Christopher and Dana Reeve Paralysis Research Center will continue to provide information and answers to the many questions and difficulties that arise when living with paralysis.

To me, the fact that Chris got out of bed every day at all was heroic when you consider that simply *breathing* was a luxury for him. Although he was forced into stillness, he never stopped going forward. Chris taught me to see that a tragedy can also reveal unknown wells of strength and how that strength, in turn, can lead to unexpected opportunities to create a life deep with meaning and worth. What a tremendous gift he left for me—and all of us. Christopher Reeve is my hero.

Dana Reeve

Paul Rusesabagina

In the spring of 1994, Hutu extremists took to the streets of Rwanda, systematically massacring their minority Tutsi and moderate Hutu neighbors. For three months, the luxurious Mille Collines Hotel became home to more than 1,200 Rwandan refugees, hiding to save their lives and those of their families. Paul Rusesabagina is the hotel manager who used his wits, international contacts, and negotiating skills to keep the refugees safe.

His story is told in the motion picture Hotel Rwanda. *Paul's second name, Rusesabagina, is a warrior name meaning "warrior who disperses his enemy and is victorious." Most people will agree that he has lived up to it. Almost one million Rwandan Tutsis and moderate Hutus were murdered during the 100-day genocide, but all 1,268 of the refugees Paul Rusesabagina fought for and sheltered, including his Tutsi wife and four children, survived.*

I have two heroes. My first hero is my father, Rupfure Thomas; the second, Nelson Mandela.

My father is the one who shaped my life. He taught me to try to be honest and sincere with my neighbors and friends. For as long as I can remember, I saw that people needed my father. When there was trouble in the neighborhood, they knew they could call him.

When I was growing up in Rwanda, there was a system for settling disputes called justice in the grass. A group of elders would meet and sit under a tree and discuss dilemmas in the village. In Rwanda many of the disputes are about land or property and the tribunal of elders would contemplate these arguments and then my father would come and solve them. The people in the village would tell me, "When your father comes, he will solve this problem." Everyone always knew what he would say: the truth.

Sometimes people who were swearing falsely would hear he was coming and suddenly confess! This was the power of my father. He was straightforward with people. He became my hero.

He was also known to speak for both sides when there was a dispute. Though he was a very eloquent speaker, he was also a very good listener. Because he listened sincerely, people in the village trusted that he would make the right decision.

Later, I went to university and got a degree. There they taught me a basic principle of business administration: If you listen, you have already solved one-half of your problem. But I already knew this. I had learned it in the grass, at the knee of my father.

My father taught me that if you want a lasting, serious life, you've got to be honest. We say in Rwanda, "You can eat from a lie once, but not every day." A person must eat every day. The truth is essential.

My father was not only generous with his wisdom and guidance, he also built trust in the community by sharing what he had with the people who needed it. Many people came to our home. My mother would give milk to the neighbors who didn't have cows and food to those who were hungry, and that was very well known.

My father paid close attention to everything around him, especially his children. Even as married adults, all my siblings would gather at my father's house on New Year's Eve. He would give us his reflections on our progress. "You have not come far enough. You have done well. You are halfway." He was very frank with us. He had nine children but he knew exactly where each of us stood. His close attention taught us things we didn't know about ourselves. We respected him. He was tough, but we were not afraid of him. My relationship with my wife is very like the relationship my father had with my mother. They were together for 49 years, until my mother died. In a marriage, each partner negotiates for his or her rights, and each partner must both give and take. My father was good at those negotiations as well!

My father's lessons have followed me. The way he educated me is the way I try to educate my children. My father used to tell us, "Whoever does not talk to his father will never know what his grandfather has said." To my father, dialogue was most important. To convey a message, to talk, was a privilege.

My other hero is Nelson Mandela, whom I read about as a young boy in school.

The first and most important lesson I learned from Mandela is to never change your message. From 1946 up to now he has been consistent in his message, fighting for rights but also respecting other peoples' lives. Black rights have been his focus, but it is very important to his success that he also respected whites. He saw South Africa to be a land for whites, for blacks, for Chinese, for Indians—a land for everybody.

Later on, when he was given power in 1994, he knew he was old. That was his pride, to be a leader of South Africa, but he also knew how to give power to others. I so admire such character. Mandela is someone who was consistent in telling people, "You have your rights, but so do we have ours." Looking at the truth. Being fair.

Mandela has fought for his rights and the rights of all people since he was very young. Even in jail he never changed his positions. I'm not sure I could do that. I have not had such a baptism.

But I felt that both those men were with me during the genocide, my own moment of truth. I had no other choice but to stay and help—my father would never have run from such a situation! I only did what he would have done. And I hope that I stood my ground, as I learned to do from Nelson Mandela.

The genocide broke out on the night of April 6, 1994. The next morning I had 26 neighbors who came to hide in my house. At first we thought the war would only take a week or a few days. So they came to stay in my house, where they felt safer.

When soldiers came to take me to the hotel, I knew immediately that I could not leave my neighbors behind. My only choice was to convince the soldiers that my neighbors were my family members.

I told them, "You can take me to the hotel, which is a good idea, but I cannot leave my family here."

On the road we were stopped by the same soldiers, who threatened us. I said, "I know you are thirsty, you are hungry, and you are tired. You are stressed by this bloody war, but do you believe the enemy you are fighting is this old man? Is this baby? Do you see yourself ever moving through this life with this baby's blood on your hands? What will be your profit for this killing? If you were to face history today, what would you say?"

We came to a compromise and I was able to take my family and my 26 neighbors up to the hotel with me.

When I had the opportunity to leave the Mille Collines Hotel where I worked, I had to make the hardest decision I have ever made in my life. I knew that some of us were going to be evacuated. I looked at those people in the hotel, the refugees—there were about 800 people by that time, and more were coming. I looked at them. I saw that I was the first person to be evacuated, yet I was the only one who could deal with the militia in favor of the victims. If I was evacuated, there was a possibility that I would not be killed. And if I was not going to be killed, I wondered how could I live afterwards? How could I live if I leave these people behind and they are killed?

I gathered my wife and my children and told them, "Listen, tomorrow, you will be evacuated." And they said, "You or we?" and I told them, "I am not going to be evacuated." I said, "If I leave this place and these people are killed, I will never eat and feel satisfied. I will never drink and feel satisfied. I will never go to bed and sleep. I will always feel guilty." I said, "Please accept my decision and leave."

I escorted my wife and children to the trucks. I helped them onto the trucks and I saw them off. That was heartbreaking and a very hard decision to make.

By the time the last truck was leaving, the radio was already reading the list of people who were on the trucks getting evacuated. I heard the execution order for my family. I heard them mention my wife by name. I heard them mention my son Tresor, who was only one and a half years old. They were saying, "All the cockroaches are leaving. They are escaping. They are being evacuated by the U.N. from the Mille Collines Hotel. Among the cockroaches that are leaving, there is one called Tresor Rusesabagina. He pretends to be going to Belgium. And yet he is not going to Belgium! He is going behind the RPF line and coming back to attack us!"

This they said of my son who was only one and a half years old.

My family and the other evacuees did not make it more than two kilometers from the hotel. They were stopped and they were beaten. Most of them were injured, including my wife. By the time she got back she was not even able to get up. She was just lying down like a dead person. But she lived, as did everyone who took refuge in the Mille Collines Hotel during the genocide.

Imagine you are driving through your village, hearing the sounds of people being killed and seeing the corpses of neighbors you know very well. You say, "There is Paul. There is Peter!" And someone comes to you and says, "You traitor! You are lucky we are not killing you today. But have this gun and kill all these cockroaches here. Remove this infestation." And the cockroaches are your wife, your children, your neighbors.

You have no choice in this moment. You simply begin to take action, to talk. And so I did. I never want to fight with guns or with machetes. I want to fight with words. You sometimes win, you sometimes lose, and through this, you learn to recognize and respect and sometimes win over the other party. My father and Nelson Mandela were both men who proved that dialogue is the most powerful weapon of all. I learned this lesson from them, and their strength gave me strength, even as I looked into the worst face of humanity.

Dennis Smith

*A*lthough he had already retired from a distinguished career as a New York City firefighter, Dennis Smith rushed to volunteer at Ground Zero on September 11 when he heard that two planes had crashed into the World Trade Center. He worked tirelessly in the days and nights that followed, and continued to participate in the recovery efforts for months afterward.

It was a single act of heroism in a life characterized by them. Smith spent many of his eighteen years as a firefighter at one of the city's busiest firehouses in the South Bronx, one of its most blighted neighborhoods. He is the author of San Francisco Is Burning, *the bestselling* Report from Engine Co. 82, *and* Report from Ground Zero, *which chronicles his own experiences as well as those of other rescue workers in the aftermath of 9/11. With those books, he has established himself as a powerful advocate on behalf of emergency workers, the brave men and women who took center stage on September 11 when they became icons of*

goodness and heroism to the world, just as the attack itself repre-
sented the purest face of evil. That advocacy has culminated in
the founding of First Responders Financial, which will provide
financial and insurance services exclusively to first responders
and their families.

The last thing in the world I am is a hero. But I *know* heroes.
I have lived among them and traveled troubled and uncer-
tain roads with them. I have laughed and cried with them. I
have stood girder straight in long lines of blue at the funerals,
and crawled with them on filthy floors through blinding
whirls to reach the red of fires. I have witnessed them running through the streets, guns drawn, shooting, praying they
would not be shot. I have knelt beside them in gutters, hand-
ing them packaged needles and bantam bottles of drugs from
their green plastic cases, along with large rolls of gauze to
wipe blood spills of possible and unknown contamination.
The street pros. The first-to-arrives—the men and women
who often guard the gate between the sad stillness of demise
and the wonderful movement of living.

Look at any photo or video of a natural or a man-made catastrophe, any terrible and deadly event from Maine to California, and study the people at the scene. Look closely at
them. Who are these men and women moving, carrying, lift-

ing, and treating with such resolve—men and women who can go from situation to situation and know what to do when tragedy and chaos strike?

My firehouse in the South Bronx, when I worked there, was the busiest firehouse in the world—thirty to forty alarms every day. There were always people on the other side of those big red doors who needed help of some kind, and we firefighters weren't the only ones willing to give everything we had to get the job done—in fires, car wrecks, home and work accidents, collapses, explosions, overdoses, shootings and knifings, that left stricken citizens lying helpless on sidewalks. There were always people willing to intercede, to mitigate: the police officers separating us from the criminals, the emergency medical technicians delivering the shock of life, the nurses in the backs of ambulances choosing the treatment of the ailing—all men and women who showed empathy, respect, and love toward strangers, just as they would for their own families.

These are people who have internalized the importance of competency. They know themselves. They have confidence in the person they see when they look in the mirror. They know the drills of triage, of decision making, of going the extra step—the sense of purpose that inspires them every time the 911 call is answered and the alarm goes out. And, in their work, many of them will see the divide between life and death, and realize that the extra step will lead them into the dangerous and unknown. Some of them will not come back.

When I was a young firefighter I got to know one man in my firehouse. In watching him I was able to set the standard for my life's work, and to this day, he symbolizes the true meaning of heroism in my mind. A tall man, he had great strength, and was always first at the door with his tools. The lock or the barricade did not matter, this man would force the door open in seconds, because like the rest of us he knew that seconds might make the difference in making a save. And, then, no matter the heat or the smoke, he would find a way to search every room that wasn't entirely in flames. Often, he would find someone and either carry or drag them out. The mayor pinned medals to his chest. In the down times, this man always made us laugh. He knew the power of levity in bringing people together. He believed in the group ethic, and was among the first to not only scramble the eggs for lunch, but also to stand before the sink afterward and wash the pot.

When one of the guys died in the line of duty one busy afternoon in the South Bronx, I was stunned to see how my role model reacted. We had been to funerals together before, but never had duty taken one of our own, in our own firehouse, and he wept openly and fiercely. This tall, tough firefighter allowed his body to shake with grief for all of us to see, and I realized that he was making the connection that I would internalize forever, the communion between what a man stood for and what the loss would mean for his wife, his parents, and his children. That day, the sadness of that family began its certain journey through our firehouse, through all the firehouses, and throughout the city. A first responder had given a life, and we all understood that it was given for us, to keep us safe.

Duty begins with the heart and a kernel of caring, and grows into action—action that is sometimes heroic. Most of us have this capacity within us, but not many of us are asked to call upon it. More than anyone, our first responders are asked to depend on their concern for others, a challenge that endures sometimes through decades of service. Our firefighters, EMTs, nurses, and police officers receive no great recompense for their work, yet they somehow buy homes, cars, and college educations for their children. They work second jobs. They vote. They don our country's uniforms and fight in foreign deserts to defend us, and our towns and cities, and our ways. They are in almost all ways average Americans. They differ only in that they are positioned on the line that separates the rest of us from harm and tragedy. And, if you need them, they will hold that line, sometimes without reason and sometimes in great peril, to protect you.

I was at the World Trade Center and watched our first responding men and women on 9/11. On that terrible day

343 firefighters, 23 police officers, 11 registered nurses, and 6 emergency medical technicians gave their lives. They and their families have given and will continue to endure much to keep us safe. Since then in America, about 150 law enforcement officers and 110 firefighters have given their lives in the line of duty. It is a big price we pay to face guns and fire, terrorism and natural catastrophe. My hero? America's first responders—they leave no great wealth in their path, but they do leave us the memory of their character, and a legacy, when it matters most to us, of being brave.

Jeni Stepanek

There is nothing so tragic, so contrary to the natural order of things, as the death of a child before a parent. Jeni Stepanek has endured this agony, not once, not twice, but four times.

Ms. Stepanek lives with mitochondrial myopathy and uses a power wheelchair for mobility. Despite doctors' reassurances that each subsequent child would be healthy, the infant-onset form of her disease led to the early deaths of three of her children. Her fourth and youngest child, Mattie J. T. Stepanek, was Jeni's "unintended miracle," and when he, too, was diagnosed, Jeni devoted everything she had to building a medical and spiritual support team for this enormously gifted and loving child.

From the start, Jeni encouraged Mattie to express his feelings in words, and showed him how he could use poetry not only to cope with his own challenges, but also to share his tremendous joy for life with the world around him. By the time he was twelve years old, Mattie had published five New York Times*–best-selling books of his poetry and had shared that poetry on* Oprah *and* Larry King Live. *Millions of people heard Mattie's "Heart-songs," and were moved, comforted, and inspired by his words. Indeed, his contribution continues even after his passing with two new books,* Reflections of a Peacemaker: A Portrait Through Heartsongs *and* Just Peace: A Message of Hope.

We would all be proud to claim a life as rich and full as the one Mattie achieved during his too brief thirteen years in the world. Since his death, Jeni Stepanek's message of compassion continues to touch the lives of millions of people around the globe who have come to know and cherish her and her young son. She recently completed the editing for Mattie's final two manuscripts, and she is currently completing a doctorate in early childhood special education with a specialization in anticipatory grief. Her mission is to help children with disabilities, their families, and the caregivers and professionals working with these children and families to cope with their unique challenges and embrace the courage, hope, and faith that made her own son's life a beacon to us all.

My hero is Mattie J. T. Stepanek—my son, and my best friend in the world. Through Mattie's innocent and uncensored expressions about life as he saw it and felt it and shared it in his "Heartsongs" poetry and other words, I have been inspired to think more deeply about my own life. Sometimes it takes the wisdom of a child for adults to really appreciate what we *do* have in life, and to remember to celebrate the gift of every day.

My hero, my son, my best friend is no longer here with me in body. Mattie died on June 22, 2004, just weeks before his fourteenth birthday. Because of his disability and intensive medical needs, we were almost constant companions. We shared thoughts and hesitations and hopes over morning coffee and afternoon tea. We shared laughter and memories over word games and board games and practical jokes. We shared hugs and tears and respect and appreciation for life and for each other in so many moments. It has been said that Mattie and I were so close we were like two people with but a single spirit. I miss that part of my spirit.

I have lived what seems like an eternity of moments without my hero, my son, my best friend, yet I look out toward the future and know that an eternity of eternities still awaits me. Each day that I have lived without Mattie is like the beginning of another "forever" all over again. And the easiest thing to do would be to lie down in the ashes of my life without Mattie, and die. But I can't, and I won't.

I can't because, before my son died, he made me promise him that I would do whatever I could not to give in to sorrow and grief and the agonizing weight of an empty lap and empty arms. And I won't because I learned from my son that we create our own epitaph and legacy—or as he called it, "the echo and silhouette of our essence"—through every choice we make in every moment of life with which we are blessed . . . even if some or many or seemingly all of those moments come filled with challenges and burdens and the pain of loneliness. And so I will try to find reasons to be truly thankful and hopeful in whatever moments may grace my lifespan, and I will strive to honor my son by continuing to "touch the world gently" in his memory.

I will go forth, carrying his "message of hope and peace" with a humble pride, and I will "always remember to play after every storm" because of my hero: Mattie J. T. Stepanek—my son, and my best friend in the world.

Vivian Stringer

*W*omen's Basketball Hall of Famer C. Vivian Stringer had more than a glass ceiling to clear in order to achieve that milestone. When she was in high school, girls were prohibited from participating in organized sports altogether, and in Springer's native Pennsylvania, a state law blocked them from trying out for the boys' teams. So the only way for Stringer to stay close to the game she loved was to become a cheerleader.

Although she wasn't allowed to play the game herself, she went on to lead a legion of women basketball players to the heights of victory. Springer is heralded by her colleagues, her players, and her opponents as one of the finest minds in the game, and she is known not only for nurturing her players but also for encouraging them to contribute to the community around them. She has won three national Coach of the Year awards, and is only the fourth Division I coach ever to win 700 games. She is the only coach in women's or men's basketball to take three different schools to the Final Four. And as coach of the U.S. Olympic *women's basketball team, she helped her team bring home the gold from Athens. C. Vivian Stringer blazed the trail so that now women can get out on the courts not only to play, but also to win.*

My mother made sure that all of us kids knew, practically from birth, that our dad was the hero. She was forever singing his praises, *"Your dad this . . ."* and *"Your dad that . . ."*

My dad was a coal miner, but he wouldn't *ever* talk about the coal mines, except to say that they were no place to make a living. I knew they were cold because he'd wear winter clothes in the summer. I knew there were rats and water in them from things that I read. I knew the men would work for hours in a bent over position from what I saw on television. And, in Edenborn, Pennsylvania, everyone knew that the wail of the sirens meant there had been an explosion in the mines. But every day, my dad would come home, his clothes filled with soot, a steel bucket in his hands, and a smile on his face.

There were six of us Stoner kids (Stoner was my maiden name), and when we weren't playing music or addressing our schoolwork, we were cleaning the house. We children often joked that our parents had kids just to clean the house and have a band! My dad, Charles Stoner, was a gifted musician who played the organ on weekends. He shared a stage with Ray Charles once, and when musicians came through Pittsburgh they'd call our house and ask, "Buddy, can you come play a gig?" He was asked to go on a tour once, but there were five kids then and it wasn't steady income, so he said no. I know it broke his heart because music was his passion, but instead of being bitter, he continued to push us to be good students in the classroom and to play music. He often played in our music room, where we had an organ, piano, sax, trombone, clarinet, flute, and even pots and pans. Our family's musical renditions entertained our community. Many times, people would sit on our porch and listen to our family play under my father's direction.

One night on his way home from a show he ran out of gas. As he walked back to the car from the service station, he dropped the gasoline can on his foot. Some time later, while he was playing the organ, he realized that his foot had never properly healed. The doctors were puzzled, and eventually he developed gangrene. He was 43 when they had to take off his right toe, then his foot, and then his leg to the knee. Ultimately, both of my father's legs were amputated.

My dad could have been so negative, but from the day his legs came off, he started to rehab. After a year of hard work, my father was back in the coal mines, back to playing the organ, and back to driving a specially modified car. I would often hear my father's muffled moans from the pain in his legs, but each morning he would go to work to provide for our family, never missing a single day.

My father inspired all of us to be our best. He taught us to take care of one another as brothers and sisters and to appreciate that family was the most important thing we had. He was the one who led our weekly family meeting when we discussed the events of the week, and he made sure that everyone got their two cents in, be it about who wasn't drying the dishes or who had had to clean the bathroom twice in a row. He was the one who told us that people have to respect you for who you are, and that we should be the best at anything we pursued. My father taught us to be open-minded, taking us to studies with Jehovah's Witnesses, into a Jewish temple, and out to a Baptist church. He was the one who'd come home in all that soot every day and wash it off, meticulously cleaning his nails. He'd put on perfectly starched pants and make sure all of us children knew to carry ourselves a certain way.

When he passed, my dad was 45, and I was 21. We had all lost the man who was everything to us, the rock of the family. But then my mom just picked up the weight.

She got a job at a supermarket, she figured out how to support us on one-fourth of the income, and she carried on, never complaining. Seeing my mom so strong made me see why my dad always told me to be independent and to be my own woman. I understood why my dad told me never to marry someone just to be taken care of and to make sure I married someone who loved and respected me on equal ground.

When I met my husband Bill, he was all of those things. He allowed me to be me. We met on a basketball court. We played field hockey and tennis, and rode bikes together. He was so proud of my work as a basketball coach. My husband was brilliant in his own right, attending medical school for three years. I am what I am because of the love and support my husband gave me. Nothing was as important as our life together as a family—husband, wife, and three happy children.

Due to our daughter's meningitis, which caused her to be a quadriplegic when she was 14 months old, my husband and I had the most unique and unifying relationship that any two people could ever be fortunate enough to have. We were happy to do whatever we needed to do to keep our family whole and happy. We didn't have the traditional husband and wife roles. My husband was just as likely to cook a meal or style our daughter's hair as he was to mow the lawn, woodwork in the shop, or play football with our boys.

When I lost my husband suddenly, I appreciated, perhaps for the first time, just how special and courageous my mom really had been. We both lost our husbands, twenty Thanksgivings apart, almost exactly the same age when they passed. It really broke me. I stayed in denial for a long time. I didn't even talk about it for ten years. But I realize now that it was my mom's example that enabled me to go on.

I had three kids when my husband died. My mom had six. I had basketball to bury myself in. She didn't have anything but us kids. And yet, we never saw her cry, we never saw her break down. My mom made it her mission to carry on our dad's lessons—and to work. My mom became the real rock of the family. There have been so many times that I wanted to give up, but then I think about my mom. I think, "How can *I* break?" My mom's example gives me the strength to know I can make it.

She's 77 years old now and she's still working. She lives in Atlanta and I'm trying to get her to come live with me, but she's too fiercely independent to take me up on it.

People are always talking about the influence my dad had on us. Just after this last NCAA Tournament, a childhood friend called me and said, "Buddy would've been real proud of you." But it's my mom, Thelma Stoner, who's been my living example. It's my mom who inspires me today.

She still says, "your dad was brilliant, your dad this . . ." and "your dad that . . ." I finally said to her a little while ago, "Do you know who *you* are? You're my hero."

My mom said in a startled voice, "Really?" I saw a smile on her face, and I pray that she knows that I meant it.

Rob Warden

*I*magine that you've been convicted of a crime that you did not commit, and face a life sentence in prison—or one on death row. It sounds like a nightmarish thriller plot, but such miscarriages of justice do happen, and with shocking regularity. Tragically (but not coincidentally) they happen most frequently to the poor, uneducated, and disenfranchised in our society—those least able to defend themselves.

That's where Rob Warden comes in. Formerly an award-winning journalist whose investigative work exposed the wrongful convictions of innocent people (including six who had been sentenced to death), Warden is now a courtroom crusader, anti–death penalty advocate, and the executive director for the Center on Wrongful Convictions at the Northwestern University School of Law.

There, Warden fights not only to overturn individual cases of legal incompetence and corruption but also to expose the systemic problems that unfairly tip the scales of justice. His commitment *is to correct those aspects of our criminal justice system that do an injustice to us all.*

The story I am about to tell brings to mind a novel I first read as a teenager—Harold Bell Wright's *The Shepherd of the Hills*, set in the Ozarks, where I grew up. "In the hills of life," the novel begins, "there are two trails. One lies along the higher sunlit fields where those who journey see far, and the light lingers even when the sun is down; and one leads to the lower ground, where those who travel, as they go, look always over their shoulders with eyes of dread, and gloomy shadows gather long before the day is done."

My story is that of a young prosecutor, an assistant Illinois attorney general named Mary Brigid Kenney, who in the early 1990s found her way to the higher sunlit fields, while her superiors, one after another, chose the trail leading to the lower ground. She stood alone in the face of intense pressure to perpetuate a horrible injustice in an emotion-charged case, with the life of an innocent man hanging in the balance.

Born in 1962, Mary grew up in a tranquil Chicago suburb near the line separating the state's two largest counties, Cook and DuPage. In her youth, she had an affinity for Nancy Drew and Agatha Christie, and dreamt of a career as a prosecutor. She realized this dream when she was hired by the Cook County State Attorney's Office after graduating from law school in 1989. Two years later she jumped at an opportunity to move to the Illinois Attorney General's Office, where she would be defending convictions on appeal in the higher courts—perhaps even the Supreme Court of the United States.

Indeed, her first assignment at the Attorney General's Office had the potential to carry her into that stratosphere. The case was known as *People v. Cruz*. Although the crime that gave rise to it had occurred more than eight years earlier, in 1983, Mary recalled it vividly. It had been terrible—the rape and murder of a ten-year-old girl in DuPage County.

In 1985, Rolando Cruz had been convicted and sentenced to death for the crime. The conviction rested on dubious testimony by DuPage County authorities who swore that Cruz had told them he had a dream about the crime—a dream that the prosecution said amounted to a confession. Cruz's jury accepted that, but eight months later a serial killer named Brian Dugan confessed that he alone had committed the crime. Unlike Cruz's purported dream, Dugan's confession seemed ironclad—rich in detail that only the killer could have known.

By all rights, Cruz should have been exonerated at that point, but other forces seem to have been at work. His exoneration would surely have been embarrassing for the authorities involved in the case, including the state's attorney—

who had political aspirations. The conviction stood, depite Dugan's confession.

However, Cruz won a new trial on appeal as a result of judicial error in the original trial. *Again* he was convicted and sentenced to death. Again, he appealed the conviction.

It was at this point that Mary Brigid Kenney was assigned to the case. She believed strongly in the integrity of law enforcement and assumed that any allegations of police and prosecutorial misconduct swirling around this case were either unfounded or greatly exaggerated. "I thought nothing so bad could happen in our justice system," she would reflect later. "This is the United States. We have a Bill of Rights."

Yet after Mary read the voluminous record of the case, it was apparent to her that an innocent man had been railroaded onto death row. She turned to her colleagues for advice, but found no comfort there. The only suggestion was to write a weak brief—and hope for the best. But she could not abide by that. "I knew it was terribly wrong," she recalled recently. "I started to wonder what kind of people I was working with."

She wrote a memo urging the attorney general to acknowledge error in the case, paving the way for Cruz to get yet another trial, but to no avail. Mary concluded she had no choice but to abandon the career to which she had so long aspired.

"I cannot sit idly by as this office continues to pursue the unjust prosecution of Rolando Cruz," she wrote in an impassioned letter of resignation, emphasizing that the case had been "infected with many instances of prosecutorial misconduct."

The appeal was assigned to another lawyer in the office and nine months later the Illinois Supreme Court, to Mary's great consternation, affirmed the conviction. But the story still wasn't over, thanks in large part to Mary. As a result of Mary's courageous stance, intense attention was now focused on Cruz's case, both from the media and from the community. The deans of six Illinois law schools and a group of prominent former prosecutors filed friend-of-the-court briefs in support of a rehearing for Cruz. In 1994, the Supreme Court bowed to the pressure and reversed the conviction, awarding Cruz yet another trial—his third.

As the trial approached in 1995, DNA technology had advanced sufficiently to link Dugan—and Dugan alone—to the crime. The trial commenced nonetheless.

The trial ended abruptly, however, when a DuPage County sheriff's lieutenant admitted on the stand that officers who claimed to have informed him of the dream statement at the time Cruz supposedly made it could not in fact have informed him, because he was on vacation. An incredulous judge acquitted Cruz, removing him from legal jeopardy after eleven years, thirty-four weeks, and four days behind bars for a crime he did not commit. In 2002, Cruz received a gubernatorial pardon based on innocence.

It should be noted that heroes like Mary Brigid Kenney are rare in positions of authority in the criminal justice system. In the hundreds of wrongful conviction cases I have investigated over the last quarter century, I have seen official after official with the opportunity to do the right thing, but who chose a lower road instead. Were that not the case, if integrity and independence were the rule rather than the exception—Mary Brigid Kenney would be ordinary, and I would not be telling her story.

As much as she might prefer it otherwise, however, she is extraordinary and deserves the highest accolade for her courageous stand in the Cruz case, a reminder to prosecutors everywhere that their responsibility is not to win or defend convictions but to do justice.

After leaving the Attorney General's Office, Mary began a rewarding career championing the legal interests of abused and neglected minors and disabled adults. Like the heroine in Harold Bell Wright's novel, she found the light lingering long after the sun had set.

Rob Warden

Elie Wiesel

Ten years after his liberation from Auschwitz, Elie Wiesel began writing about his experiences of the Holocaust. What emerged was Night, *a memoir that offers one of the most powerful insights into life and death within the barbed wire confines of the concentration camps.*

Wiesel grew up in a tight-knit Jewish community in Sighet, a small town in Transylvania. The Nazis came to Sighet in 1944 when Wiesel was 15, and all Jewish citizens were deported to concentration camps in Poland; he never saw his mother and younger sister again. Wiesel and his father managed to stay together in the camp until his father's death in the last months of the war.

After the war, Wiesel emigrated to France and, ultimately, to New York City. Since then, Wiesel has worked ceaselessly to promote understanding and equality, and to defend the causes of persecuted people throughout the world. He won the Nobel Peace Prize in 1986 for his efforts to defend human rights. He and his wife, Marion, used the prize to found The Elie Wiesel Foundation for Humanity, to "advance the cause of human rights by creating forums for the discussion and resolution of urgent ethical issues."

Wiesel's ongoing mission as a teacher, speaker, writer, and humanitarian is to make sure that the world never forgets the devastation of the Holocaust, and to remind all of humanity that we must never again remain silent when horrific crimes are committed.

I am deeply skeptical about the very concept of the hero for many reasons and I am uncomfortable with what happens in societies where heroes are worshipped. As Goethe said, "blessed is the nation that doesn't need them."

To call someone a hero is to give that person tremendous power. Certainly that power may be used for good, but it may also be used to destroy individuals.

Which societies have proven to be the most fertile fields for the creation of heroes, and have devised the most compelling reasons for hero worship? Dictatorships. Stalin and Hitler were worshipped as gods by millions. It was idolatry, or worse, blind faith. Anyone who questioned the gods, knew too much, or rebelled in any way was finished.

Even if we do not worship our heroes, they may cow us. It takes a certain amount of confidence and courage to say, "I can do something. I can change this and make a difference." But if you, as a writer, think, "What are my words next to those of my hero, Shakespeare?" then something is lost for those who need your help and your voice. Excessive humility is no virtue if it prevents us from acting.

So we need to be very careful of those we put on a pedestal, and choose only those who embody those qualities that reflect the very best of human nature. But even that is a dangerous game. What do we do with a hero who has done something less than heroic?

None of our forefathers was perfect. Moses is probably the single most important figure in the Bible besides Abraham. He was a teacher, the leader of the first liberation army, a legislator. Without him, there is no Jewish religion at all. Yet of the many things he is called in the Bible, he is never called a hero, perhaps because he did not always behave heroically. He began his public career by killing an Egyptian; later, he failed to identify himself as a Jew. For these reasons and others, he is prevented from entering the Promised Land with the people he has led there. Is Moses a hero?

Is a hero a hero twenty-four hours a day, no matter what? Is he a hero when he orders his breakfast from a waiter? Is he a hero when he eats it? What about a person who is not a hero, but who has a heroic moment? In the Bible, God says, "there are just men for life and there are also just men for an hour." Is a just man for an hour a hero? The definition itself and the question of who deserves the title are slippery at best.

I do believe in the heroic act, even in the heroic moment. There are different heroisms for different moments in time. Sometimes just to make a child smile is an act of heroism.

In my tradition, a hero is someone who understands his or her own condition and limitations and, despite them, says, "I am not alone in the world. There is somebody else out there, and I want that person to benefit from my sacrifice and self-control." This is why one of the most heroic things you can do is to surmount anger, and why my definition of heroism is certainly not the Greek one, which has more to do with excelling in battle and besting one's enemies.

My heroes are those who stand up to false heroes. If I had to offer a personal definition of the word, it would be someone who dares to speak the truth to power. I think of the solitary man in Tiananmen Square, who stood in front of a column of tanks as they rolled in to quash a peaceful protest, and stopped them with his bare hands. In that moment, he was standing up against the entire Chinese Communist Party. I think of the principal cellist of the Sarajevo Opera Orchestra, who sat in the crater formed by a mortar shell blast and played for twenty-two days—one day to commemorate each one of his neighbors killed in a bread line on the same spot—while all around him, bullets whistled and bombs dropped. Those people were heroes.

Maybe heroes can simply be those people who inspire us to become better than we are. In that case, I find my heroes among my friends, family, and teachers. My mother and father's respect and love for learning had a great influence on me, and my son's generosity and humility continue to inspire me.

It was my grandfather who allowed me—who obliged me—to love life, to assume it as a Jew, and indeed to celebrate it for the Jewish people. He led a perfectly balanced life. He knew how to work the land, impose respect on tavern drunks, and break recalcitrant horses, but he was also devoted to his quest for the sacred. He told wonderful stories of miracle makers, of unhappy princes, and righteous men in disguise.

When I was a child, my heroes were always anonymous wanderers. They experienced the wonder of the wider world and brought it to me in my small village. These men were masters. A master must give himself over to total anonymity, dependent on the goodness of strangers, never sleeping or eating in the same place twice. Someone who wanders this way is a citizen of the world. The universe is his neighborhood. It is a concept that resonates with me to this day.

In fact, it is to one of those wanderers that I owe my constant drive to question, my pursuit of the mystery that lies within knowledge and the darkness hidden within light. I would not be the man, the Jew, I am today if a disconcerting vagabond—an anti-hero—had not accosted me on the street in Paris one day to tell me I knew nothing. This was my teacher Shushani Rosenbaum. He said he spoke thirty languages, and there wasn't a country he hadn't visited. He looked like a beggar.

I was his best student, so he tried to destroy my faith by demonstrating the fragility of it. This was his chosen role: the troublemaker, the agitator. I gave him my reason and my will, and he shook my inner peace, destroyed everything I felt to be certain. Then he built me back up with words that banished distance and obstacles. Learning this way was a profoundly disturbing experience, but a life-changing one. I have never stopped questioning and challenging what I believe to be true. I speak of him as a disciple speaks of his master, with tremendous gratitude, and his is the advice I give to young people: "Always question."

In Hebrew there is no word for hero, but there is one that comes close, based on the word for justice: *tzaddik*. A *tzaddik* is a "righteous man," someone who overcomes his instincts. In the ancient texts, this would mean sexual instinct, the life force, but of course it can be extended to all the emotions connected to that force: jealousy, envy, ambition, the desire to hurt someone else—anything, essentially, that you want to do very much.

There is a story about a *tzaddik* that says a great deal to me about the character of the true hero. A man came to Sodom to preach against lies, thievery, violence, and indifference. No one listened, but he would not stop preaching. Finally someone asked him, "Why do you continue when you see that it is of no use?" He said, "I must keep speaking out. In the beginning, I thought I had to shout to change them. Now I know I must shout so that they cannot change me."

Elie Wiesel

Acknowledgments

Grateful doesn't even begin to capture the depth of our joy at working with such a talented and dedicated group of people to produce this book. This complex but worthwhile project wouldn't have happened without the intelligence, charm, and tenacity of our three wise men—Bob Pritzker, Albert B. Ratner, and Michael Vlock, who have informed and supported this project every step of the way.

Thanks to each of the contributors for taking the time to share their thoughts and stories about those people who have most inspired them. By sharing these stories, you help inspire the hero in all of us.

Kudos to our tenacious and talented editor at Free Press, Elizabeth Stein, her assistant Maris Kreizman, publicity director Carisa Hays, and publicist Jill Siegel, and to our publisher, Martha Levin. Hats off to our woman of many hats, literary agent, midwife, and wordsmith par excellence Laurie Bernstein. A million thank-yous for the hard work, creativity, and dedication of the entire My Hero Project book team: If there was a medal of valor in publishing we'd award it to Laura Tucker, Kathy Crockett, and Jennifer Hixson, who were in the trenches the whole way through. We are also indebted to Deborah Hare, Charles Harper, Richard Kent, Susan Morgan, and Judith Stone for their contributions. Special thanks, too, to David Chaudoir, Brenda Jones, Dave Kaplan, Aditi Kinkhabwala, Ken Kurzon, Tipp Nunn, Joyce Oberdof, and Mark Salter.

In the words of the novelist G. B. Stern, "Silent gratitude isn't much use to anyone," so we trumpet our thanks for the support and goodwill of Jonathan Alter, Amber Bobin, Heather Brocious, Laura Brown, Patricia Burke, Rachel Burton, Anthony Carbonetti, Roxanne Coady, Chris Demouth, Conrad Erb, Colleen Fitzgibbons, Isobel Floyd, Sam Gejdenson, Naomi Graham, Bridget Groman, Laurie Hawkin, Elizabeth Hoskins, Chris Howard, Monica Hunt, Laurie Jacoby, Jack and Lynn Kearney, Jill Kearney, Marc Krizack, Richard Levin, Dan Levy, Ellen Lewis, Jonathan Liebman, Mia MacDonald, Steve Mariotti, Susan McCotter, Debra McCurdy, Janice Meagher, Linda Mehtor, Tracey Milburn, Maria Miller, Sunny Mindell, Beth Montgomery, Jamie Moore, Carole Nathan, Shelley Olson, Zoe Pagnamenta, Wendy Pinto, Ruth Pomerance, Pattie Poole, Gregory Prince, Joshua H. Reinitz, Esq., Keith Rudman, Deborah Seager, Gwen Sheehan, Jayme Smeerin, Maria Stasek, Genevieve Stewart, Mike

Stotts, Vice Admiral Edward M. Straw, Mary Jane Vero, Emily Wachtel, Elsa Walsh, Jennifer Warden, Aaron Weiler, Jeff Wilson, Judi Wilson, Darice Wirth, and Lois Wyse.

This book would not have been possible without the support of the staff at the My Hero web site. Thanks go to the devoted team that helps to produce this award-winning interactive online journal: Stephanie Cole, Margaret Dean, Karen Chu, Nathan Smith, Wendy Milette, Victoria Murphy, Antonio Mendoza, Grissel Villar, Claudia Herrera Hudson, David Kemker, Wendy Jewell, and Charles Harper. Special thanks to Dorothy and William J. Meyers, Ken Koslow, James Pelts, Jim Hawkins, Harvey and Barbara Markowitz, Peter Anderson, The Foundation for the Contemporary Family, the U.S. Department of Education, The Sloan Foundation, the Honorable Rosa DeLauro, Mark Cavanagh, Helene Cavanagh, Dan Weisman, Carl Levinson, Steve Grace at LA36, and Gary Birch and the Laguna College of Art for their ongoing support of the web site.

Thanks to television producers Tom Weinberg, Joel Cohen, and Skip Blumberg for their work on the *My Hero* pilot that is used in classrooms, after-school programs, libraries, and museums around the globe.

A growing team of educators are providing crucial feedback and assistance with the development of new tools for The My Hero Project, including Sara Armstrong, Jerrilyn Jacobs, Susanne Nobles, Marci Stein, Andrew Greene, Cheikh

Seck, Deborah Hare, Rowena Gerber, Joanne Tawfilis, Kerry Pellow, Lynn DiMatteo, Ed Gragert, and fellow educators who are part of The International Education and Resource Network. Student volunteers Slater Jewell-Kemker, Nadine El-Hadad, Riley McMahon, Charlie McMahon, Patrick Kiyemba, Madeline Jacobs, Kelly Monroe, Molly Harper, Rashid Peters, Allison Schwartz, Dana Schwartz, Abbey Trachman, and Jennifer Cole help spread the word about this project to teachers and students around the world. We also wish to thank the thousands of teachers who take part in this project and the millions of students of all ages from over one hundred nations who share their stories and provide inspiration and hope to us all.

Technical support for the My Hero web site is provided by Cashman Computer Associates: Bob Cashman, Cathy Mason, Dana Urban, and Doug Handy. Thanks to Andrea Drexelius at The Rockefeller Group Telecommunications Services and Integration Works for hosting this dynamic web site. Additional technical support for www.myhero.com has come from Kelvin Lam, Duncan McAlester, SBC Interactive, The Associated Press, the USC Annenberg Center for Communication, Jon Goodman, Ph.D., Michael Goay, and The Digital Coast Roundtable: Conchetta Fabares, Director.

This project is a collaborative effort of many talented and skilled people committed to celebrating the best of humanity by spotlighting heroes from all walks of life. We are deeply grateful to all of our heroes around the world for the hope and courage they give us to meet whatever challenges lie ahead.

Jeanne Meyers
Rita Stern
Karen Pritzker

Charitable Organizations Supported by Contributors to *My Hero*

The Abyssinian Baptist Church
132 Odell Clark Place (formerly
 138th Street)
New York, NY 10030
212-862-7474
www.abyssinian.org

Bronx Preparatory Charter
 School
3872 Third Avenue
Bronx, NY 10457
718-294-0841
www.bronxprep.org

Bulletin of the Atomic Scientists
6042 South Kimbark Avenue
Chicago, IL 60637
773-834-1810
www.thebulletin.org

The Carter Center
One Copenhill
453 Freedom Parkway

Atlanta, GA 30307
404-420-5100
www.cartercenter.org

Center on Wrongful
 Convictions
Northwestern University Law
 School
357 East Chicago Avenue
Chicago, IL 60611
312-503-2391
www.law.northwestern.edu/
 wrongfulconvictions

Christopher Reeve Paralysis
 Foundation
500 Morris Avenue
Springfield, NJ 07081
800-225-0292
www.christopherreeve.org

CJ Foundation for SIDS
The Don Imus–WFAN
    Pediatric Center
Hackensack University Medical
    Center
30 Prospect Avenue
Hackensack, NJ 07601
201-996-5111, www.cjsids.com

The Creative Coalition
665 Broadway, Suite 804
New York, NY 10012
212-614-2121
www.thecreativecoalition.org

Creative Visions
1223 Sunset Plaza Drive
West Hollywood, CA 90069
310-652-8833
www.creativevisions.org

The Elie Wiesel Foundation for
    Humanity
529 Fifth Avenue, Suite 1802
New York, NY 10017
212-490-7777
www.eliewieselfoundation.org

Erin Gruwell Education Project
P.O. Box 41505
Long Beach, CA 90853
562-433-5388
www.gruwellproject.org

The Global Tribe Network
1223 Sunset Plaza Drive
West Hollywood, CA 90069
310-652-8833
www.globaltribenet.org

Hereditary Disease Foundation
1303 Pico Boulevard
Santa Monica, CA 90405
310-450-9913
www.hdfoundation.org

Association of Hole in the Wall
    Camps
265 Church Street, Suite 503
New Haven, CT 06510
203-562-1203
www.holeinthewallcamps.org

The Hotel Rwanda
    Rusesabagina Foundation
36 Crafts Street
Newton, MA 02458
617-614-1610
www.hotelrwandarusesabagina
    foundation.org

Illinois Mathematics and
    Science Academy
1500 West Sullivan Road
Aurora, IL 60506-1067
630-907-5000
www.imsa.edu

JASON Foundation for
Education
44983 Knoll Square
Arlington, VA 20147
703-726-8279
www.jasonproject.org

Jazz at Lincoln Center
33 West 60 Street, Floor 11
New York, NY 10023
212-258-9800
www.jalc.org

The John D. and Catherine T.
MacArthur Foundation
140 South Dearborn Street
Chicago, IL 60603
312-726-8000
www.macfound.org

The John Glenn Institute for
Public Service & Public
Policy
350 Page Hall
1810 College Road
Columbus, OH 43210
614-292-4545
www.glenninstitute.org

Lown Cardiovascular Research
Foundation
21 Longwood Avenue
Brookline, MA 02446
617-732-1318
www.lowncenter.org

Magic Johnson Foundation, Inc.
9100 Wilshire Blvd., Suite 700
East
Beverly Hills, CA 90212
310-246-1106
www.magicjohnson.org/
foundation

Mia Hamm Foundation
P.O. Box 56
Chapel Hill, NC 27514
919-544-9848
www.miafoundation.org

The Michael J. Fox Foundation
for Parkinson's Research
Grand Central Station
P.O. Box 4777
New York, NY 10163
800-708-7644
www.michaeljfox.org

The Muhammad Ali Center
One Riverfront Plaza, Suite
1702
Louisville, KY 40202
502-584-9254
www.alicenter.org

Muhammad Ali Parkinson's
Research Center
500 W. Thomas Road,
Suite 720
Phoenix, AZ, 85013
602-406-4931, www.maprc.com

The Nature Conservancy
4245 North Fairfax Drive,
    Suite 100
Arlington, VA 22203-1606
800-628-6860
www.nature.org

New York Police & Fire Widows
    & Children's Fund
Stephen J. Dannhauser,
    President
c/o Weil, Gotshal & Manges
767 Fifth Avenue
New York, NY 10153
212-310-8326
www.nypfwc.org

QuestBridge
P.O. Box 20072
Stanford, CA 94309
650-566-8391
www.questbridge.org

RP International
P.O. Box 900
Woodland Hills, CA 91365
818-992-0500
www.rpinternational.org

The Rudolph W. Giuliani
    Trauma Center at
    St. Vincent's Hospital
130 West 12th Street, Suite 1-G
New York, NY 10011
Phone 212-604-7554
Fax 212-604-7533

SattelLife
30 California Street
Watertown, MA 02472
617-926-9400
www.healthnet.org

Scott Hamilton CARES
    Initiative
The Cleveland Clinic Taussig
    Cancer Center
9500 Euclid Avenue/R36
Cleveland, OH 44195
800-440-4140
www.scottcares.com

Small Planet Institute
25 Mount Auburn Street,
    Suite 203
Cambridge, MA 02138
617-441-6300, ext. 115
www.smallplanetinstitute.org

The Troubadour Foundation
610 Fernhill Road, S3, C40
Mayne Island, BC V0N 2J0
Canada
250-539-3588
www.troubadourfoundation.org

United Cerebral Palsy
1660 L Street, NW, Suite 700
Washington, DC 20036
800-872-5827, www.ucp.org

Wangari Maathai Foundation
Kenya: P.O. Box 67545
00100 Nairobi, Kenya
011 254 20-251-333 ext. 686
London: c/o The Gaia
    Foundation, Kate Povey
011 44 207 428-0055
www.wangari-maathai.org

Whirlwind Wheelchair
    International
San Francisco State University
1600 Holloway Avenue, SCI 251
San Francisco, CA 94132-4163
415-338-6277
www.whirlwindwheelchair.org

Women's Sports Foundation
Eisenhower Park
East Meadow, NY 11554
800-227-3988 (U.S. only)
516-542-4700 (business)
www.womenssportsfoundation
    .org

Yogi Berra Museum & Learning
    Center
On the Campus of Montclair
    State University
8 Quarry Road
Little Falls, NJ 07424
973-655-2378
www.yogiberramuseum.org

Tell the World About *Your* Hero!

Do you have a hero story that you would like to share with us? Since 1995 visitors to our web site have been invited to share their stories, and we would like to extend that same invitation to you. If you have a story about a hero who has inspired you or touched your life in some way, please share your story with us.

Some stories will be selected for publication in future My Hero books or for posting on our web site. If your story is chosen for publication you will be credited.

Please send your stories to:
www.myhero.com
The My Hero Project
"Hero Submissions"
1278 Glenneyre
Laguna Beach, CA 92651

In addition, the MyHero web site welcomes your photos, artwork, and short films (five minutes and under). For more details, visit www.myhero.com.

About The My Hero Project

The My Hero Project is a not-for-profit organization whose mission is to inspire the hero in all of us by shining a spotlight on real-life examples of people at their best. The three founders are as follows: **Karen Pritzker,** formerly a magazine editor, works as an advocate for literacy and children's issues. She served as editor for this book. **Rita Stern** is an artist and Emmy Award–winning documentary filmmaker and was an architect of the original MyHero web site. Her artwork is exhibited in fine-art galleries around the country. **Jeanne Meyers** is a film and multimedia producer who helped develop and has continued to direct the award-winning MyHero web site since its inception in 1995. She is passionate about global storytelling and the use of new technology to effect positive change in the world.

www.myhero.com is a leading site for parents and educators, with its accessible curriculum and user-friendly interactive media literacy tools. The site encourages reading, writing, and computer literacy skills. The site affords an intimate and supportive connection between teachers in disciplines as diverse as English, technology, civics, and science, while also connecting children throughout the nation and the world, making it a valued teaching tool in more than 20,000 classrooms.

About the Introduction Author

Earvin "Magic" Johnson, bestselling author of *My Life,* is universally known for his illustrious thirteen-year career with the National Basketball Association. Since his retirement, he has redefined himself as a businessman with the objective of revitalizing and providing quality entertainment and services to neglected urban communities. The Magic Johnson Foundation focuses on addressing and improving the health, educational, and social needs of inner-city youth, and on supporting related charitable organizations.